ESSEX AND SUGAR

More than any other county, Essex has been the
stage for some of the outstanding events in
English sugar history.

Essex and Sugar

Historic and other connections

by

FRANK LEWIS
A.R.Hist.S.

With a Foreword by
Lord Lyle of Westbourne

PHILLIMORE

1976

Published by

PHILLIMORE & CO. LTD.
London and Chichester

Head Office: Shopwyke Hall,
Chichester, Sussex, England

ISBN 0 85033 107 2

Printed in Great Britain
by W & J Mackay Limited, Chatham
by photo-litho

TO

MY WIFE

CONTENTS

Chapter   *Page*

     Illustrations ix

     Foreword xi

I   Honey in Essex 1

II   Cane Sugar comes to Essex 14

III   Cane Sugar 1700-1860 23

IV   Essex Admirals and the Sugar Islands 35

V   Essex and the Sugar Slaves 46

VI   Essex and Slave Emancipation 62

VII   The Silvertown Refiners 1:
     Duncan, Tate, Martineau 76

VIII   The Silvertown Refiners 2:
     Lyle, beginning and end of a great refinery —
     Tate and Lyle 88

IX   Beet Sugar and Essex 100

X   Other Sugars and other Matters 112

     Sources of Information 124

     Appendix 130

     Index 131

LIST OF ILLUSTRATIONS

(between pages 52 and 53)

Plate
1. The Hon. Samuel Barrington

2. The French Fleet attacking the English Fleet in St. Lucia Bay

3. The Old Refinery, Sugar House Lane, Stratford

4. Bee Boles, Eastbury House, Barking

5. 'Forecaster', Beet-harvester

6. Outpost of Bee Farm, centred at Mayland

7. Beet Factory, Felsted

8. The Tate Gallery, London

Figure
1. Token of John Parker, Romford, 1669   34

2. Sugar Factory, Antigua, in the 18th century 87

FOREWORD

Early Days in Essex

From 1917 till 1925 I lived with my parents at Coopersale Hall. I was aged between 12 and 20 years, and the period covered my time at Harrow School and Cambridge. Consequently I was only there for the holiday periods and certainly enjoyed life there.

We had about 12 acres of land and my father had a small farm with dairy cattle and pigs. The surrounding country was beautifully rural in those days, considering our distance from the centre of London (about 15 miles). This was no doubt helped by the slow train service in those days (nearly one hour between Liverpool Street and Epping).

I have not revisited the area recently, and there are doubtless many changes.

LORD LYLE OF WESTBOURNE

PREFACE

Fifty years in a Silvertown sugar refinery, followed by another eight years assisting in guiding visiting parties around the refinery, and an even longer period as a lover of rural Essex and later student of the county history have enabled me to perceive the remarkable connections between Essex and sugar in the remote and immediate past. More than any other county, Essex has been the stage for some of the outstanding events in English sugar history. That this was little known was evidenced by the usual response of surprise when I have mentioned that I was studying the history of sugar in Essex, which has suggested to me that here was a gap in county and sugar knowledge that might usefully be filled, hence the attempt in this book. Some connections may seem to be strained to breaking-point, but are included for their interest. Technicalities have been kept to a minimum, and sufficient background from beyond Essex is provided to give fuller understanding of the county data.

The many sources of information are acknowledged at the end of the book, and to them I express my indebtedness. Particular mention must be made of the Essex Record Office, the British Museum Reading Room, the reference library at Water Lane, Stratford, the *Tate and Lyle Times* and its editors. Assistance is also acknowledged from members of the Havering libraries staffs, particularly Mr. R. Chartres, from Mrs. and Miss Root, Mr. E.A. Berry of Manbre and Garton, Mr. R. Powell, editor of the *Victoria County History of Essex,* Messrs. J. Watson (of Tate and Lyle) J. Green, C. Quinton-Tullock and others who have helped. Authors and publishers have been kind in permitting quotes from works. Lord Lyle's kindness in contributing a foreword was much appreciated.

Most of my notes on the several sugar industries apply as far as the end of 1970, since when have occurred other changes in processes and organisation.

F. LEWIS

CHAPTER I

HONEY IN ESSEX

MOST PEOPLE when asked to think of sugar, would picture in their minds the familiar bowl of granulated or cube on the tea table. But this, whether processed from sugar-cane or sugar-beet, has a more specific name, sucrose, and is but one of a large number of sugars in constant use by man, such as glucose, lactose (in milk), maltose (in malt) and others. Figuring amongst them is honey, perhaps the most interesting historically, for it was the principal sweetening agent known for a great period of time in the past, in some countries the only sugar available. The bee appears on tomb, statue, or picture of Egypt 6,000 years ago, and in a cave painting of Valencia, Spain, dating back 4,000 years, a Neolithic man is shown clinging to a wall of rock while robbing a honey-store, bees hovering round menacingly. The classical Greek writers make many references to bee culture and honey production, while familiar are the numerous mentions in the Bible of Nature's sweet gift, on two of which can be made an Essex commentary. The Promised Land of the Israelites was of one flowing with milk and honey, and this delectable vision of pasture and blossom has been applied to our county by an ancient writer, Norden, who in 1594 alluded to Essex as the English Goshen, 'the fattest of the lande', comparable to Palestine that flowed with 'milke and hunneye'. Also with an Essex reverberation is the story of the Bible's strong man Samson, who slew a young lion and found later in the carcase bees and honey,[1] suggesting the famous riddle 'Out of the eater came forth meat, out of the strong came forth sweetness'. The episode of lion, bees and honey provided an appropriate trademark for a well known Silvertown food product, Lyle's Golden Syrup, the religious side of the early Lyles helping them in the difficulty of choosing a suitable subject.[2]

To sweetness from the strong of claw was added sweetness from the strong-sounding by John Whittier, the American poet, whose tenuous Essex connection is discussed later; he has a poem 'The Hive at Gettysburg' in which he moralises on the homing of bees in 'a stained and shattered drum' left from the battlefield, its beating to war replaced by the hum of the honey-bee.

The Romans great beekeepers, favoured hives of wicker and clay, the Saxons disposed to wattle construction, and a third innovation, hives of straw drawn up to an elongated top point, was introduced into Essex and the rest of East Anglia by the Danes.[3] In the Saxon economy the bee ceorl was a servitor of some value, providing the sole means of sweetening and also the base of mead, the heady drink. After the conversion of the Saxons to Christianity, he rendered a third service, the candles for the church from his beeswax, for this substance does not melt in hot weather as does tallow[4] and is aromatic when burnt; also a halo of reverence shone round the flame, for the bee had acquired a sacred significance as in the legend of St. Ambrose (340-397). When an infant, a swarm of bees settled on his lips; the terrified nurse was prevented by the father from disturbing them, and presently the bees flew high up and out of sight, the babe unharmed, interpreted as a sign of future greatness, which indeed followed. He, however, shares this indication of divine favour with other famous, Plato for instance. St. Ambrose appears in stone, painting, or glass in some East Anglian churches. A short-lived Essex example[5] was in the Tillingham church when in the 1890s the Rev. W. Miller put in a stained-glass window, behind the vicar's stall, showing the saint holding a hive with its circling bees. It was destroyed by fire in 1935 and replaced by one of different character.

From the sphere of legend we turn to fact with the Domesday Book of William the Conqueror. It is most fortunate that of two sections into which the book was divided, the lesser section examined separately the counties of Essex, Norfolk and Suffolk and enumerated amongst the other possessions of the manors, the beehives where they existed. In the

larger book covering the rest of England the commissioners
ignored the hives, probably deciding that a listing of effects
so minute as to include such items was too large a project,
after their experience with the surveying of the three counties
above. So in these counties, with the livestock of the manors
— horses, cattle, swine and the like — figure the beehives, the
products of such deemed of sufficient value for them to be
noted, and that they receive any mention at all in the great
Survey underlines the importance attached to beekeeping in
Saxon and Norman times and its place in the manorial
economy. The total number of the hives in the three counties
were Essex 615, Norfolk 467, Suffolk 359, giving our county
the leading position in the craft of bee ceorls. These figures
represent the hives farmed for the manor lord, and would
not include the odd rough hives about the dwellings of villein
or cottar.

The disposition of these bee colonies in Essex, raising
questions of why such situations and numbers, accounts for
130 apiaries, of the following capacities:-

23 hives, Shortgrove near Newport.

16 hives, Thaxted.

Over 5 hives, 35 manors, including Berwick in Rainham 12,
and Barking 10.

5 hives, 13 manors.

4 hives, 17 manors.

3 hives, 27 manors (including east Hamme).

2 hives, 29 manors (as examples, Thundersley, Walthamstow, Wickford, Ugley, Ulting).

1 hive, 11 manors (as examples Great Warley, Little
Wakering, East Mersea, Boxted).

What cheese-paring zeal is displayed in the listing of a single
hive! Although households of higher rank also used wax
candles in preference to tallow, some of the larger colonies
could exist to serve a church or chapel with the proper
illuminants — Barking, for instance; while at Berwick
(Rainham) a chapel existed from early times, mentioned in
the 12th century, and could have had a Saxon forerunner,
for the book states that a Saxon priest tilled a piece of ground
in the neighbourhood, and an extensive burial ground of the

late pagan period nearby could have continued with some sacred purpose with the converted Saxons. East Ham, mentioned above, is now in the borough of Newham, as also is Silvertown, so that in the great area included in the new borough, three beehives were the tiny prelude to the colossal sugar factories to arise later at Silvertown. Honey was of tempting value, and in the ordinances of Edward the Confessor, of interest to Essex people because of his palace at Havering, were punishments for stealing from beekeepers; the wild hive was guarded by the laws against poaching and trespassing.

These ancient hives of primitive materials needed protection from inclement weather, cavities in walls, termed boles, sometimes serving this purpose. The six boles at Tilty, Essex, recently recognised and restored,[6] are very interesting. Ranged in two rows of three, one row over the other, the boles are openings in a structure of mortared flint measuring 8 feet long by 5 feet high and 2 to 3 feet in thickness, which seems to have been built as a separate unit and not part of a wall, for each angle is strengthened by a rounded buttress. The arched roofs of the bole cavities are toughened with bricks. Through the introduction of Mr. A.C. Brown, hon. editor of the *Essex Beekeepers Association Magazine* I was able to see the boles, situated in a pleasant farmhouse garden. Though originally much decayed, and restored by members of the above Association, the ancient appearance is retained and gives support to a belief that they formerly belonged to Tilty Abbey, now vanished except for a portion of wall composed of flint material like the boles.

Bee bole sites in the British Isles number over 100, and among the Essex examples besides Tilty are the six boles in the Tudor garden wall of Eastbury House, Barking. They also exist at Horham Hall, Thaxsted, and Hassingbrook House, Stanford-le-Hope. I added to the Tudor list when my newly acquired knowledge of boles enabled me to recognise the nine (probably 10) in the garden walls of Bretons manor house, South Hornchurch. Hitherto, the purpose of these wall recesses had been a matter of conjecture to people viewing them, but feeling I had discovered the original use, I sent photographs and measurements to Dr. Eva Crane, of the

Bee Research Association, who informed me that all the experts there agreed they were bee boles, and the photographs were added to the Association's files. At some time in the past, one wall containing five boles had been enclosed by a lean-to greenhouse, and wall and boles coated with plaster, so that the disappearance of these in impending building operations will not be such a severe loss; the Havering town clerk has noted my request for care in preserving the remaining boles, some still in good condition, and will follow up the suggestion from Mr. R. Chartres, Librarian at South Hornchurch, that an explanatory plaque be placed on the wall.

Among the many writers of the past, on bees and beekeeping, are a few Essex names. Thomas Tusser, born at Rivenhall, near Witham, produced in 1571 a remarkable book of verse on the whole art of agriculture, *Five hundred Good Pointes of Husbandry,* covering with his four-line verses the farming year month by month. The quaintly worded but instructive quatrains do not forget the beehives:

May
Take heed to thy bees, that are ready to swarm,
the loss thereof now is a crown's worth of harm,
Let skilful be ready, and diligence sene
lest being too careless though losest they beene [bees].

September
Now burn up the bees, that ye mind for to drive
at Midsummer drive them, and save them alive
Place hive in good order, set southly and warm
and take in due season, wax, honey, and swarm.

Set hive on a plank, not too low by the ground
where herb with the flowers may compass it round
And boards to defend it from north and south-east
from showers and rubbish, from vermin and beast.

December
Go look to thy bees, if the hive be too light
set water and honey, with rosemary dight
Which set in a dish full of sticks in the hive
from danger of famine ye save them alive.

'Driving' the bees means smoking them from a full hive into an empty one, and some beneficial qualities seem attached to rosemary.

Despite such poetical advice to others he was unsuccessful
with farming in Norfolk and Suffolk. Through illness he made
a brief return to his native Essex:

> From Norwich aire in great despair
> Away to flee, or else to die . . .
> To house my hed, at Faiersted, where whiles I dwelt.

About the same time another writer, Holinshed,[7] in 1577
comments on an inferior kind of mead, made in the county.

> There is a kind of swish-swash, made also in Essex and other
> places, with honey and water, which the country wives, putting
> some pepper and a little spice, call meade, verye good in my
> opinion for such as love to be loose-bodied; otherwise, it
> differeth so much from the true methmeglyn as chalk doth from
> cheese. Truely, it is nothing else but the washing of the combes
> when the honey is wrung out; and one of the best things that I
> knowe belonging thereto is that they spend but little labour and
> lesse cost in making of the same, and therefore no great losse if it
> were never occupied.

This seems a case of damning with faint praise.

Samuel Purchas, incumbent of Eastwood, Essex, published
1657 *A theatre of politicall flying-insects,* anticipating the
scientific approach to the bee of today to supplement the
practical, giving anatomical and physiological details of bees
and such related insects as wasps, hornets, bumble bees, their
internal organs, respiration, circulation; there is a section on
the bees of America, and an account of his opening the crops
of sparrows eating his bees and finding therein only drones.
300 devout short sermons at the end of the book display his
Puritan tendencies.

His anatomical studies did not include the organ associated
by the general public with that insect almost as much as
honey — the sting in its tail, but the following Essex writer
gave special attention to this in his works. He was William
Derham, rector of Upminster 1689-1735, who combined his
religious thought with a wide interest in natural history,
astronomy, and other scientific subjects. In the wooden
belfry beneath the spire can still be seen the door of the
opening from which the rector made his observations. In
his Boyle lectures 'Physico-theology' he described in detail

the stinging mechanism of the bee with its 'two, small, sharp, bearded spears'. In 1724 he contributed an article on the mating of wasps to the *Philosophical Transactions of the Royal Society,* and though bee-mating is similar he did not proceed with such sexual studies with the bees, or he would have earned the distinction of the planned elucidation of the mystery of the queen bee's sex, solved by accident a few years later by another cleric when a queen laid eggs as she crossed his hand (Rev. J. Thorley).

The next writer connected with Essex touches upon the question of the areas of the country most favourable to the apiarist. In 1822 John Lawrence, using the nom-de-plume of Bonnington Moubray, included a bee section in his book *A practical treatise on breeding all kinds of domestic poultry,* mentioning that in 1787 honey was sold at 2d. a lb. in Hampshire and Essex and that by 1818 it had risen to 6d. a lb., which made beekeeping now profitable; he proceeds to affirm that the Braintree and Bocking neighbourhood produced some of the finest honey in England, a claim of some magnitude, for England had gained the reputation of being the leading beekeeping country.

In the years that followed most probably some Essex writers were included among those writing on bees, and one of recent years I found very interesting. In 1923 Herbert Brown, rector of St. Lawrence near Southminster, wrote *A Bee Melody.* An enthusiastic beekeeper, he produced the book, he stated, to engender a love of bees, and if subject matter both interesting and instructive, personal and local anecdotes, and a literary treatment suggested by the title can, when blended, arouse regard for these wonderful creatures, then this book should do it. His 'takes' or collected honey from hives 70 to 80 years ago have interest, as:

1881, a good season. 4 hives together yielded 200lbs.
1882, most disappointing season. 4 hives   50lbs.
1889, a very good season   6 hives   390lbs.
1893, very dry season.   6 hives negligible.
1894, cold and wet   4 hives   20lbs.
1897, a good season   5 hives   280lbs.

He records honey as 1s. a lb. In his delightful little book of sketches he mentions that Rudyard Kipling has lively verses in *The Bee Boy's Song* about 'telling the bees', of which apiaral custom more anon.

Bensusan in *Back of Beyond*, No. 47, listens while the old shoemaker sitting by his garden hives holds forth on the medicinal value of honey, points out the differently coloured tiny balls of pollen on the legs of the bees, congratulates himself on no big orchards with nasty sprays in the neighbourhood, and wishes that more men would make hives rather than armaments.

Another writer, Herbert Mace of Harlow, editor of *The Beekeeping Annual*, published in two sections, Elementary and Advanced, a most competent and exhaustive beekeeping work, which followed other writings of his on bee matters.

The mention of 'telling the bees' alludes to an ancient superstition of bee owners, that unless the bees are told of a death in the family the insects will die or disappear; accordingly they were informed and sometimes the hive dressed with crepe. As an Essex example a century ago, at Hyde Green, near Ingatestone, the answer to an enquiry after the bees was: 'They have all gone away since the death of poor Dick; for we forgot to knock at the hives, and tell them he was gone dead'.[8] As recently as 1925 writers asserted the belief still survived in many parts of the country; Stock a specific case.[9] Mr. H. Holmes of Mayland, Essex, bee farmer, has a childhood memory of crepe put on the hives when a grandfather died, the name of the deceased and the demise spoken to each hive. John Whittier (1807-1892) the American poet, has a sad little poem on the belief, and he has an interesting but slender link with Essex. He was born at Haverhill, in Massachusetts, that state containing many Essex place-names. The English Haverhill, Suffolk, formerly had a part of Essex called Haverhill Hamlet, and the county historian, Philip Morant, instances other connections. Another interesting link is that the Rev. Nathaniel Ward, born at Haverhill and rector of Stondon Massey, emigrated to Massachusetts in 1637 and formed settlements there.[10] Did he or his people bring over from Essex the old bee-telling custom which aroused Whittier's muse in this shadowed poem 'Telling the Bees'? It is the story of one who, after a long absence, hurries to the home of his beloved, where she dwells with her people, among whom is her aged grandfather.

Just the same as a month before,
The house and the trees.
The barn's brown gable, the vine by the door
Nothing changed but the hive of bees.

Before them under the garden wall
Forward and back
Went drearily the chore girl small
Drooping each hive with a shred of black.

Trembling I listened; the summer sun
Had the chill of snow;
For I knew she was telling the bees of one
Gone on the journey we all must go!

For I said to myself 'My Mary weeps
For the dead today;
Haply her blind old grandsire sleeps
The fret and pain of his age away'.

But her dog whined low; on the doorway still
With his cane to his chin
The old man sat; and the chore girl still
Sung to the bees stealing out and in.

And the song she was singing every since
In my ear sounds on:
'Stay at home, pretty bees, fly not hence!
Mistress Mary is dead and gone'!

Now from poetry to beekeeping technique, greatly advanced since the early days of the straw, wicker, wattle, or bark hives, when they were left alone till autumn, the bees then killed with sulphur fumes, the combs cut out, the honey strained from breeding remains. Nowadays the National wood hive of three storeys is the home of several thousands of bees — workers or honey bees, drones, and queen, and confines the last with her larvae to one chamber while the workers continue to deposit pure honey above; ready-made foundations for the honey combs are provided, and the bees quietened by a smoke-puffer while full combs are replaced by empty. No one who has been introduced to a hive at work as I was by Mr. D. Bond, chairman of the Romford branch of the Essex Beekeepers Association, will afterwards remain indifferent to a bee among the flowers, with its wonderful instincts.

The mention of Romford, in the wide area of which are about 100 hives despite its urban character, again poses the question which are the most favoured Essex areas for the bee, a good district considered three times the value of the less endowed. As chalk and limestone districts have this superiority, the best places for successful beekeeping should be in the north of the county. But there can be exceptions to this rule, an example being the surprisingly large yields of light-coloured clover honey from a patch of clay country near Saffron Walden, but rarely obtainable a few miles away. Though some parts of the county are more favoured, beekeeping can be practised in all areas, as witness the eight divisions of the Essex Beekeeping Association, Braintree, Chelmsford, Colchester, Epping Forest, Maldon, Romford, Saffron Walden, Southend-on-Sea, covering the whole of the county.

Mr. A.C. Brown informs me that even in the suburban area of Manor Park he has collected 1½ cwts. from one hive, much accounted for by large numbers of nectar-yielding sycamore and lime trees within easy flying distance for the bees.

Manor Park prompts the insertion here of the honeyed nomenclature grouped in a not distant area. Essex has a district so well endowed with apiaral names that it must be unique in the country. Beehive Lane in Ilford, a busy thoroughfare, has known rural days. In it in 1609 a mansion house stood named 'Le Beehive'. The Chapman and Andre Map, 1777, shows two areas with cottages near the Lane named Great Beehive and Little Beehive, and these dwellings or their successors appear in the Silver Street and New Street cottages to be described below. G.E. Tasker in his book *Ilford Past and Present* (1901) writes 'Beehive in 1796 was a farmhouse in the forest. There was formerly a mansion of that name which had been the seat of the Fullers and Osbalde-stons. The small village of Beehive near Valentines derives its name from the old house.' The 1929 street directory of Ilford still used this name 'Beehive' for the district, and lists there two groups of 'Beehive Cottages'. One row numbered 1 to 8 stood in Silver Street (now Radnor Crescent), a turning off Beehive Lane near the *Beehive* hotel. These have disappeared. From Radnor Crescent a passage way leads into

Inglehurst Gardens, which runs between Beehive and Red-bridge Lanes. The Redbridge Lane end was listed in the 1929 directory as 'New Street, Beehive' and contained a second row of Beehive Cottages, numbered 1 to 7 (now incorporated in Inglehurst Gardens and numbered 45 to 71.) These are on the site of the 1777 Little Beehive dwellings. The present cottages have been modernised, but retain somewhat the older appearance. The wall-plate with the name 'Beehive Cottages' still shows; at the other end of the row appeared on the cottage walls a concrete plaque in the shape of a beehive, and when taken down during renovations, it was salvaged by Mrs. Joyce White, Bee Disease Officer for Herts., who now displays it in front of her residence at Bury St. Edmunds. Of course at Beehive there is a cafe so named, and there is also a Beehive school. In conclusion one wonders whether Essex alone among the counties possessed a 'village' named simply Beehive.

The bee gathers nectar from the blossom and converts to honey in the hive, and white clover heads the list of nectar-yielders, while other familiar wild flowers yield a largesse of sweetness; also the lime, the willow aswarm in spring, and other trees; the bees at the blackberry bush long before the berry-pickers; the farmer's crops and the orchards both giving to and needing the pollinating creature; the cottage gardens like an emergency ration. The big beekeepers will sometimes transport their hives from clover to heather country to gain the thick dark honey.

The spraying of crops presents the problem of injury to bees just when they are increasingly needed for successful cultivation of field and orchard, for the ploughing up of grasslands, the destruction of hedges, the inclusion for cultivation of hitherto unregarded odd corners and patches, all incidental to modern farming, have eliminated pollinating insects with the wild flowers and blossom that supported them, including the chief of pollinators, the wild or bumble bee, unable to find nesting places. Pollination by insects is essential for fruit growing and for many crops, and because of the destruction listed above a demand for hive bees has

arisen and the migratory beekeeper with his transportable
hives plays an important part in modern farming. In Essex[11]
are 13,000 acres of orchard and 2,000 of soft fruit, and
hundreds of stocks of bees are taken there in blossom time,
but as spraying could be lethal for the bees, there is need
for co-operation between grower and apiarist about times of
spraying. This could be assisted by the work of May & Baker,
the well-known manufacturing chemists of Dagenham and
Norwich, who have a research station at Ongar, Essex. Here
among other inquiries are those concerning spray insecticides,
a facet of which is the study of their toxic effect on bees, reports of which could be helpful in arrangements between fruit-
grower or farmer and beekeeper during spraying time. Dr. D.
Twinn, in charge of these investigations, informs me about a
dozen hives are kept at the station for observation.

Most hive-owners practise as a hobby, but among them
are the professional or semi-professional bee farmers, and
Herbert Mace in 1952 compared Essex with neighbouring
counties concerning such commercial establishments. Taking
40 hives as a minimum for such undertakings, Essex and
Surrey each had two bee farms of 40 to 200 hives, Suffolk
three of similar capacity, while Kent with its orchards had
five of that size, two of them possessing 200 to 400 hives.

I visited in 1968 an Essex business of this kind, that of
H.W. and R. Holmes of Bicknacre Grange, Mayland, described
in advertisements as 'Migratory Apiarists' dealing in 'Bees for
pollinating, Honey, Beeswax, Nuclei, Stocks and Swarms'.
With the explanatory guidance of Mr. H. Holmes, here was
spent a most rewarding day. To give sufficient range for the
many thousands of bees the hives on a bee farm are widely
spaced, and with Mr. Holmes and friends I inspected the
separate colonies of about 10 hives situated in secluded places,
sometimes in different parishes. From Althorne was a view
across the Crouch valley, over which the bees would travel if
a tempting arable crop appeared on the opposite side (which
spacious travelling reminded me of a rent exacted by the
ancient landowner of the bee owner for use of flowers, the
rentable area fixed by how far church bell or cock crow could
be heard). We learnt our host had won a County Shield in

the National Show, with other trophies. The average hive yield was 30 to 60 lbs. per season, but he had touched 160 lbs.; 20 hives had given him a ton in a year; to feed the bees used nearly a ton of sugar during the year in syrup form. an economical feed for bees being a 'denaturised' sugar, especially prepared. His honey found sale in Southend-on-Sea. his bees polinated orchards in such places as West Bergholt, Hawkely, and Chelmsford, in which orchards the hives would remain some days or up to three weeks.

The Essex Beekeepers Association, part of the National Association, arranges conferences, lectures, practical demonstrations, and shows. It is estimated that 6,000 hives exist in Essex. As a specimen year, 1952, the E.B.K.A. figures are presented — average yield per hive 37.3 lbs., Harwich best with 56.2, Epping lowest 29,2 lbs.; Saffron Walden lost highest place; there were 32 instances of over 100 lbs. from a single hive; the best in the Clacton area 290 lbs. and Chelmsford 250 lbs. The total honey that year with a good honey flow in the county, was 45,397 lbs. from 1,217 colonies among the membership of 900.

Mr. A.C. Brown, now of Little Canfield, Dunmow, in his comments on the above figures, is of opinion that in those areas much affected by the considerable change in the pattern of agriculture since 1952, which has lessened very much the foraging capacity of the bee, for instance in the Dunmow district and the Rodings, the average yield per hive is around 25 lbs. The revival in the popularity of mead is noticed in wine shows.

As I pass on from the honey story to that of cane sugar, heeded is a warning from Joseph Conrad, the Polish-born author whose first married home was Stanford-le-Hope, and who in his *The Inn of Two Witches* writes: 'It was a dull-faced manuscript — a treatise on Sugar Refining (the dreariest subject I can think of) could have been given a more lively appearance'.[12]

CHAPTER II

CANE SUGAR COMES TO ESSEX

FROM THE 12TH CENTURY honey was increasingly supplanted by cane sugar as the chief sweetening substance in Britain. Long before it reached these shores it had been known in the East, growing wild in south-east Asia, receiving mention in Indian literature of 500 B.C., and the soldiers of Alexander the Great in 300 B.C. reported 'reeds of honey though no bees'. In 74 B.C. the Roman Pliny the Elder writes of sugar from the cane as 'white and brittle' suggesting that solid sugar is being produced, and as its use spread to the Mediterranean countries around 600 A.D. there is mention of the cane juice boiled to promote crystallization.

It is considered that its introduction into this country was helped by the Crusaders bringing back, as a pleasant novelty for their women, samples of the new sweet substance, and from this period the trickle of sugar from East to West increased to marketable flow, though for a long time to remain a luxury of the well-to-do. At first sugar showed only in royal accounts, and a first Essex linkage is in the household expenses lists of Eleanor,[1] wife of Simon de Montfort and sister of Henry III. During the several months of 1265, when her husband was nearing the end of his fatal conflict with the King in the 'Barons War', Eleanor was first at Odiham Castle, near Basingstoke, then sought the greater safety of the castle at Dover. Her sojourn here has Essex interest. Two manors of the county, South Hall in Rainham and Dovers in Hornchurch, have links with the castle; South Hall once in its barony and contributing to its defence, Dovers taking its name from the owning family descending from the Norman warden of the castle who assumed its name for his own, de Dover. The busy roundabout of Dovers Corner continues the name.

But a closer Essex link is that the steward of the de Montfort estates was Sir Richard of Havering. Among the purchases of the countess in this troubled time were:
For 12 lbs. of sugar, 12 shillings
For 6 lbs. of powdered sugar with mace, 6 shillings.
She comments that between April and June the price of sugar rose from 1s. a lb. to 2s. a lb. Hardly surprising with civil war raging! The above prices must be increased to astronomical proportions to match today's monetary values, and because of its rarity and cost sugar was included in the spice list by the great households and, as we see above, was often mixed with spices; white sugar was imported in the form of 'loaves', cone-shaped, which were broken into convenient pieces or powdered by pestle and mortar.

Sugar, syrups, and treacle or molasses were prescribed medicinally in early days, and an odd allusion to this appears in the work of Thomas Lydgate,[2] born near Clare, Suffolk, about 1370. In his writings of the life of St. Giles, the 7th-century saint, it is claimed there was a special cult of this saint in Essex, and one of the several tales of him is that concerning the king who had such a grievous sin upon his conscience that he feared to confess and asked the saint to pray for him. This was done, and later appeared on the altar a scroll promising forgiveness after penance. Lydgate likens this conscience-salving to medical easement

And as thou wert treacle and medicine
To King Charles, when he in mischief stood.

Treacle and brimstone were long a curative for children's complaints.

In the Elizabethan period, the accounts of Sir John Petre's household at West Horndon, Essex, showed on Christmas:[3]

	£	s.	d.
For one loaf of fyne sugar at 20d. per pound	1	5	8
For one loaf of the second sugar at 14d. per pound		16	10

These items make the loaves approximately 15 lbs. each, and also indicating grading. Other Petre items elsewhere are March 1580, pound of sugar 17d., and also are ordered around this time 11 lbs. of fine sugar 14s. 8d., 9¼ lbs. of fine sugar

at 19d. per lb. 14s. 7d., and 1 lb. at 14d. These items were
listed under Dyett (diet).

In the currency of those days and for a period afterwards
the prices reveal how costly sugar was still and made any
quantity an acceptable gift for dignatory or cleric in order to
thank, please, or ingratiate. Some illustrative items are given.[4]
From the 1588 accounts of St. Christopher-le-Stocks (on the
site now occupied by the Mansion House, London):

> For 4 sugar loffes for the judges   £4 10s. 0d.

From All Saints, Derby 1639-40

> For a sugar loff 12 lbs. 3 ozs. for the minister   £1 0s. 0d.
> For 2 sugar loves 15 lbs. 12 0zs. for the minister   £1 2s. 6d.

Essex examples of such sweet gifts occur when William
Hall, Colchester Chamberlain, in c.1629 presented the Earl
of Sussex with:

> Two sugar loaves at 18d. per lb.   29s.

His presentation to the Lord Bishop (Harsnett) was:

> Sugar, 25 lbs. at 18d. per lb.   33s. 6d.

Smaller amounts, such as 2lbs., were included in other gifts
to the Earl and to the High Sheriff by the Maldon Chamberlain
in 1564. In the early accounts of Sir William[5] (father of Sir
John), Secretary of State and builder of Ingatestone Hall,
it is surprising to find a 1543 item of this price:

> Sugar and Spice — sugar 60lb. at 7d. a lb.

The ordinary selling price seems to have been lowered for
Sir William. The association of sugar with spice seen above is
repeated on the occasion of Queen Elizabeth's visit to Ingatestone Hall in 1561:

> Sugar, cloves, mace, pepper, and sundry other kinds of spice (etc.)

In 1550 an interesting small purchase was made, presumably
from the village shop, for Lady Petre:

> Laid out for sugar candy at Ingatestone for my lady — 2d.

As part of his official duties, the great Secretary shared in
the task of dissolving the monasteries, after which came the
turn of the chantries and churches for confiscation. Petre

possessed property in Devon, where he had been busy among the monasteries, and when church plate was being appropriated for the Crown from that county came the gift of sugar loaves to the Secretary and the Earl of Bedford with conciliatory intent.

A member of the noted county family of Barrington, Sir Thomas, was one of the 'knights of the shires' representing Essex in Parliament for some years till 1640, when to serve certain Puritan interests he consented to be returned in the less exalted position as member representing Colchester, which entailed much residence in Great Queen Street, London, instead of Hatfield Broad Oak. While there, certain acceptable food and other gifts arrived from county acquaintances, including in February 1642, three sugar loaves[6] from the Mayor of Colchester. Great Queen Street (off Kingsway) has a public house named the *Sugar Loaf,* and as in Sir Thomas's time there was a Sugar Loaf Court in the street, there may also have been an inn of that name, a forerunner of the present place of refreshment (which has an 1832 reference). Hardly possible that all this prompted the Mayor's gift!

The Barrington family had a sweet tooth,[7] for while the widowed Lady Joan Barrington was residing at the Priory, Hatfield, in 1620, such items as these occur in the household accounts:

For 1 lb. of lump sugar	14d.
For a sugar loaf	8s. 2d.
For 20 lbs. sugar and box @ 13½d. per lb.	23s. 4d.

and these may have been used in conjunction with

For 2 lemons	13d.
For 1 lb. brimstone	4d.

In 1660, the family disbursements for things sweet are: 27 June, 3lbs. of sugar at 1s. per lb. for

preserving raspberries	3s. 0d.
For a lb. of sugar	1s. 0d.

4, 11, 27 May, 3, 23 June, for each date

1 lb. of sugar	10d.

Later on three successive days, the purchases were 1 lb. of sugar, 10d., 3 lbs. of sugar for raspberries, 1 lb. of sugar, 10d. The price of sugar thus varied from 10d. to 1s. 0d. a lb., in the later lists, and still is high 20 years later, for the young housewife May Aylmer of Mowden Hall[8] near Ulting, leaves records of purchases in 1680 including:

> 2 lbs. of sugar 2s.

The relative dearness of sugar is realised when other items are listed:

20lbs. of beef	4s.
11 lbs. of cheese @ 3d. per lb.	2s. 8d.
1 oz. of pepper	2d.

The sugar 'loaf' so often mentioned derived its distinctive shape from the early method of obtaining white sugar. The prepared molten sugar was poured into cone-shaped moulds arranged points downward, and as it hardened into crystalline consistency, cleansing syrups were passed through which drained from a hole in the mould's point; after a long period of drying the now solid cone of sugar was removed from its mould, and sold thus to grocer or large customer.

Despite its cost, high because of the cumbersome, long, and expensive production of those days, use of sugar was spreading, and the loaf appearing in more shops and homes — in fact, the sign indicating a grocer's shop usually depicted sugar loaves. In the 17th century, the loaves appeared on coins known as 'tokens'. During the first two Stuart reigns the scarcity of small value coins was causing public inconvenience, made worse when from 1649 to 1672, all minting of copper currency ceased. Towns, authorities, tradesmen and the like made arrangements for the issuing of token coins for their own use in the immediate neighbourhood by private mints. Made of brass, copper, or tin, of different shapes but mostly round, the tokens often show or state the business of the issuer, and those of grocers of Essex bearing the sugar loaf are:[9]

One Sugar Loaf

Billericay,	Edward Rhett	Farthing	No date

Blackmore	Robert Peachey	Farthing	No date
Braintree	John Hanwicke	Farthing	No date
Colchester	Christopher Bayles	Farthing	No date
Colchester	Thomas Bayles	Farthing	No date
Ilford	William Kempeton	Farthing	No date
Kelvedon	Richard Sedley	Halfpenny	1669
Romford	John Parker	Halfpenny	1669
Romford	James Scott	Halfpenny	1668
Romford	Thomas Steevns	Farthing	1651

Three Sugar Loaves

Chelmsford	John Bastable	Farthing	1657

Sugar Loaf and Clove

Brentwood	John Beetes	Halfpenny	1669

Sugar Loaf and Merchants Mark

Coggeshall	Edmund Spicer	Farthing	No date

In this and the following century the sugar loaf often appeared in the long arrays of shop signs displayed in the principal London streets, usually triple, and sometimes in conjunction with apparently unrelated objects, e.g. 'The Dolphin and Three Sugar Loaves', which might be explained by the signs of two shops combining into one when one shop disappeared. Not only grocers but also inns sported the sweet loaf signboards, still an Essex example at Sible Hedingham, *The Sugar Loaves*. An address befitting a fairy tale would be:

Sugar Loaf House,
Cuckoo Lane,

a house so named and situated showing near North Stifford on the Chapman and Andre Map of Essex, 1777. Despite search, little or nothing is known of it, the last appearance on the O.S. 1 in. map for 1844,[10] and it stood approximately on the site of the present Chalk Pit Farm, opposite the still existing Cuckoo Lane. The elfin-sounding abode reminds me that when in London in search of Sugar Loaf Court, unable to locate it but knowing that I was near, I asked a young clerk if he could direct me and he replied he could not but thought it sounded like Alice in Wonderland! The name 'sugar loaf' was applied to white conical hats, rounded or pointed at the

top, worn by people in Tudor and Stuart times, the shape
persisting into the traditional clown's headgear. My son's
Boys' Country Book of 1839 describes a collection of old
hats brought out for wear in a school walk, 'pudding-
crowns, square-crowns, and even sugar-loaf-crowns such as
Guy Faux himself wore'. (More about sugar loaves in
Chapter 10).

From where came the first precious sugar? Egypt, Syria,
Sicily sent their freights of cane sugar, passing through the
chief trading port, Venice. During the journey from the
sugar factories to the city of canals the sugar sometimes
suffered deterioration, or poor product would arrive, which
led to a second processing or refining at Venice, for which
factories were built. England began to receive and refine
these Mediterranean sugars herself with, in 1544, the
erection of a refinery in London by Cornelius Bussine,
increasing to 50 the following century. The second processing
or refining of sugars from the cane-growing countries became
an established practice in sugar production, this final finishing
in the country of sale proving to have many advantages. The
now regular course of operations was for the factory in the
plantations to express the sweet juice from the canes by
rollers turned by a windmill or circling cattle, this juice
clarified by lime or other substances while boiling and, when
thick enough to crystallize when cool, poured into hogsheads
to harden and drain for a considerable period, then shipped
to the refining country. On receiving this 'raw' sugar, the
refiner melted it into a syrup, which again was subjected to
cleansing substances, among which agents bullocks' blood or
eggs sometimes figured, the coagulation of these substances
embracing the impurities in the syrup, which rose to the
surface of the boiling mass as scum, to be continually skimmed
off. This operation was repeated three or more times in a
range of open coppers or 'pans', the syrup ladled from one
to the other till it was clarified sufficiently for the final
concentration, after which it was poured into moulds as
already described.

A rich new source of sugar began when Christopher

Columbus discovered the West Indian islands in 1492, and introduced sugar cane culture to them. The first English colony was St. Kitts, 1642, followed shortly after by Barbados, in which settlement the sugar cane was introduced about 1642, to become the principal crop and to earn the island the name 'Mother of the Sugar Islands', though its area is little more than that of the Isle of Wight. The increased planting of cane in the three decades 1656-1686 considerably lowered the price of sugar for England, carrying its consumption into classes other than the rich. For plantation cultivation a large and permanent labour force was needed which could be acclimatised to prevailing conditions, and later we shall see how this want was satisfied by African negro slavery. But labour for these early planters was first supplied by white workers of low or fugitive standard — political or criminal offenders, the debtor, the desperate or the fortune-hunter, royalist exiles, prisoners-of-war, the pauper, the rebel, and the inevitable Irish. The forced migrants could have the prescribed 10-year terms of labour increased as punishment for some offence against rules, and their welfare was less regarded by the planter than that of the purchased slave, his own property. Such conditions awaited some prisoners of the Civil War and of the uprisings before and after; were any Essex unfortunates among them? A search through John Hotten's work *The original lists of Persons of Quality, emigrants, religious exiles, political rebels, serving men sold for ten years, apprentices, children stolen, maidens pressed, and others who went from Great Britain to the American plantations 1601-1700,* a truly inclusive title, discovered no Essex people, but a gap occurs in the records from 1630 to 1673, a period including the Civil War, when it could be expected that royalist prisoners would be transported. That exile and bondage to the sugar plantations for war prisoners took place is shown in this extract about the Monmouth rebellion unfortunates:

> Mr. Rose's list. Invoice of 68 men servants shipped on board ye 'Jamaica Merchant', they being to be sold for ten years in Barbadoes or Jamaica, December 9th, 1685.

For possible Essex prisoners of the Civil War treated thus
the siege of Colchester 1648 should give some examples.
The Rev. G.F. Townsend[11] writing of the surrendered when
the siege ended states: 'The Londoners . . . were for the most
part sent to Bristol to be transported [to Ireland] or as
slaves to America, or some other colony or plantation'.
Bristol for long was the leading slaving port before losing the
dubious distinction to Liverpool. Thomas[12] Cromwell (1825)
quoted an early writer, M. Carter, on the siege prisoners 'and
some were sold (as before they did the Scots) to be transported into foreign countries'. A.C. Edwards in his *History
of Essex* has a statement that General Fairfax 'transported
many prisoners to the West Indies', and another annalist
'Many were sold for service in the plantations'. V. Harlow
who partly fills the time gap in Hotten's work with *A History
of Barbados 1625-1685,* remarks that whenever Cromwell was
at loss to know what to do with an awkward character
he almost invariably ordered transportation to Barbados.
Colonel Gardiner, Major Thomas, and other royalist officers
were sent to Barbados after imprisonment in the Tower, which
brings us to the Essex family of Ayloffe.

Among the royalist officers who came out of the besieged
city to surrender was Colonel William Ayloffe, who later
escaped. He was the son of Sir Benjamin Ayloffe who
was owner of Bretons manor in Hornchurch and of other
properties, a trusted confidant of the King, and at the
outbreak of hostilities was appointed Sheriff of Essex.
Sir Benjamin's loyalty cost him imprisonment in the Tower
and sequestration of estates at the end of the war, and
Philip Morant, the Essex historian, goes on to state that
'the captive was taken from the Tower later and sent to
Yarmouth, with many more, to be banished to the Plantations
in the West Indies, but that inhuman order being reversed'
he compounded for his estates by a heavy fine, which obliged
him to sell Bretons.[13] A fortunate escape, however, from
a woeful change of rural estates and his green levels beside
the Thames for the hot plantations of Barbados.

CHAPTER III

CANE SUGAR — 1700-1860

IT HAS BEEN ESTIMATED that from 1700 to 1800 the annual consumption of sugar in this country rose from 10,000 to 15,000 tons, the increase due not only to rise of population but also to the larger average consumption per person. The 50 refineries of 1644 became 120 a century later, small family affairs each producing about 5 tons weekly, and in 1750 together they refined 30,000 tons of sugar. In 1780, two leading London refineries could process 13 tons weekly. The raw sugar cost 34s. per cwt., the refined loaf sugar sold 62s. per cwt.,[1] the difference in figures showing how costly was the process of manufacture, and the retail price would work out dear for the less affluent, also varying in localities. A London saddler[2] included in his weekly budget, 1775.

1 lb. of lump sugar	7d.
2 lb. of coarse sugar	10d.

but the accounts of the overseer for the poor in St. Lawrence, Essex in 1792[3] showed the following:

1 lb. of lump sugar for the nuss (nurse)	1s. 2d.
To a pound of sugar	8d.

These items repeated later, indicate two standards, the lump sugar pieces cut from the white sugar loaf, the cheaper variety probably a yellow moist. But the prices above must be viewed with the knowledge that a shilling in the 18th century had a much greater monetary value than one in the 19th century, and greater still than one in the following century.

The spread of tea drinking in most classes, and its sweetening, was one of several causes for increasing demand, which did not escape some criticism by Arthur Young for

one, for this author of *A General View of the Agriculture
of the County of Essex* complained thus in 1767, 'as much
superfluous money is expended on tea and sugar as would
maintain 4,000,000 more subjects on bread'. The linking of
tea and sugar is pictorially presented in some grocer and tea
merchant signs in 18th-century London, e.g. 'Tea Tub and
Three Sugar Loaves' 'Sugar Loaf and Tea Cannister' 'Tea
Chest and Sugar Loaf' 'Green Cannister and Three Sugar
Loaves'.

In the 18th century the increase of foods without con-
trolling regulations was accompanied by widespread adulter-
ation. My father was apprenticed to a grocer in the Victorian
era, when the young men 'lived in', and in my boyhood he
would amuse me with an imaginary conversation between
grocer and assistant in the closed shop on Sunday morning:
'John, have you put the chicory in the coffee?'
'Yes, sir.'
'Have you put the brickdust in the pepper?'
'Yes, sir.'
'And the sand in the sugar?'
'Yes, sir.'
'Now come to church.'

In Georgian times this was more than a joke, this sand in
the sugar, together with brickdust in the cocoa, dust in the
tea, lime in the flour.[4]

The increasing tonnage of sugar coming to London was
met by the building of the West India Dock in 1802, its
chief purpose to receive the sugar assignments. *Pigot's
Directory* for 1826-7 shows no refiners in Essex, but lists
80 gathered together in Whitechapel, Mile End, St. George's
and the vicinity. But an Essex link appeared in the fact that
some of these refiners had chosen to live east of the Lea
river.

Recently I toured the East End districts, with names and
addresses taken from the Directory above, but did not find
a single survivor of these numerous enterprises — forgotten
too as I discovered at the local history room of the central

library. Yet sugar refining was once the staple industry of the East End before it was largely gathered into Silvertown. 'In the East End streets about 1860 could be seen all hours of the day great wagons containing 6 hogsheads of raw sugar, each 5 tons, and drawn from the docks by a fine breed of carthorses on the way to the refineries, and on the other side of the road a much longer line of smaller wagons or carts for delivering the refined product to customers. 'Across East London the refinery chimneys could be seen'.[5] Charles Dickens writes in *The Uncommercial Traveller* (1860) of walking through the East End and passing 'the huge piles of buildings belonging to the sugar refiners'.

These refiners made five products, loaf sugar, white crushed, yellow crushed, a little brown sugar, and treacle. George Martineau gives a not unpleasant picture of bustle and interest, but another writer viewed the industry differently, as will be seen later. The numbers of these refineries lessened as the century passed, the smaller concerns supplanted by fewer larger establishments with the introduction of more effective but expensive processing and machinery, but as late as 1860 there were still 20 sugar houses here, and the larger businesses turning out 300 to 400 tons weekly.

Refiners found the Whitechapel turnpike road, and later the railway, convenient for those who wished to reside in surroundings more congenial than those around their sugar houses, and several settled in the then residential districts of Stratford and neighbouring rural areas. An early mention of Essex interest is that of John Cooper, Whitechapel refiner, who in 1737 negotiated a land deal at Little Heath, in the north end of Dagenham parish.[6] Later the 1841 census has Claus Hinkens, with a refinery in Cable Street, living at Maryland Point. From the same source in 1851 came several instances of the daily journey to the pleasant retreats of nearby Essex away from the dinginess of East London, as John Bowman, his refinery in Great Alie Street, West Ham born and living with his family at 9 The Grove; Peter Kuck of Hanover, his sugar house in Prince's Place, Cable Street, living with his Russian wife and a son who assisted him in the

business at 1 Crownfield Place; Joseph Schroder, born at
St. George's in the East, though of German descent, his
refinery at 7 Christian Street, living with wife and family at
13 Stratford Green; Martin Titgen, of Germany, his business
in St. George's in the East, with his wife at 95 High Road,
Stratford; Charles Dames, born in Whitechapel, his business in
Rupert Street, Goodmans Fields, living with wife at 70
Forest Rise, near Whipps Cross (Dames Road, Stratford, is
named after him).[7] This last fact about road naming suggests
local notoriety, though none of their names appears on the
Vestry lists for the West Ham Parish, which would include
most of these addresses, but indications later suggest that if
not in administration then in local good causes these sugar
families participated.

Farther out, Essex interest is shown by Deiderick Schwinge,
sugar refiner, Christian Street, St. Georges, who in 1854-6
owned several pieces of land at Woodford,[8] and about the
same time Ludwig Finkin, sugar baker of Whitechapel, owned
three pieces of waste land near Woodford Wells. 'Sugar baker'
could denote a refiner or a panman (of the latter more later),
and we find a 'sugar boiler' in 1841, William Saick living in
High Street, Stratford.

The involvement of people from the sugar industry in
local good works, is shown by these extracts from a local
history *Old Plaistow* (1905). Miss E. Bishop, a retired head-
mistress, describes a visit she made to Plaistow at Christmas,
1840.

> I entered the quiet and quaint little village to visit Mrs. Schroder.
> Mr. Schroder was a retired sugar refiner, suffering from paralysis
> on one side, Mrs. Schroder a kind old lady. The house was a tall
> house at the entrance of the village from Stratford. After I had
> completed my visit, they wished me to make their house my
> home out of school hours, and they made me very happy, as I
> used to read to them and could attend to the old gentleman's
> knitting, which (German-like) he did for amusement'.

Of the North Street Chapel,

> the committee was composed of Mrs. Schroder, Mrs. C. Marten,
> Miss Sturge, and the Misses Anderson. I was once asked to go and

see an old woman somewhere down a lane. Mrs. Schroder gave me some money for her as her furniture was burnt'.

The hospitality to a young teacher, committee work for the Independent (Congregation) Chapel, and aid to a distressed woman, were like forerunners of the grand scale philanthropy and public-spirited work of the great Essex refiners to come. The name Marten occurring in the extracts will receive mention again later; also that of the author of *Old Plaistow,* John Spencer Curwen.

In another (then) old-world village dwelt a retired sugar refiner, John Wagener, born in Trentelburgh, Germany, with a business in Mansell Street. In 1850 he purchased Great Langtons, Hornchurch, built about 1760, one of the largest residences in a district blessed with several, outstanding, fine houses and overlooking an ornamental lake and wide gardens. The extensive grounds included a cricket field famed for the old Hornchurch Club, which, in the closing years of the 18th century, played such teams as Essex, Middlesex, and Marylebone (M.C.C.). After his death in 1884 his wife continued to reside here till her own demise in 1891. The house then became the property of Colonel Holmes, who in 1863 had married Emilie, the elder of the Wagener daughters, so here indeed a sugar refining family through marriage was linked to social effort and public work. Henry Holmes, a ship builder and ship owner 'was one of the first to realise the approaching end of the era of the wooden ship, and to recognise the enormous possibilities of iron and steel ship building'.[9] He was also a bank director and for some years joint proprietor of the Old Hornchurch Brewery. His military rank stemmed from the Volunteer movement, for which he raised a battery of the Essex Artillery Volunteers, of which corps he became colonel and for which he built a drill hall. Ground for a new fire station and the first municipal offices were given by him. Chairman of the local bench of magistrates, Hornchurch member on the Essex County Council, his house the centre of social and political activities, leadership in the philanthropic and charitable movements in the district — in this wide sphere of public spirited work no

doubt Mrs. Wagener and other members of both families
participated. After the death of Mrs Wagener, her daughter
continued to reside here with the Colonel, and later they took
up residence in the new house 'Greytowers'. A tenuous link
with sugar continued at Langtons with the next owner,
W. Varco Williams, son of Samuel Williams, of Dagenham
Dock fame. Varco bought the house from the Colonel in
1899. He became partner with his father in the Thames-side
business, and later chairman of the company. The sugar
interest lies in Dagenham Dock where raw sugar has long
been unloaded from the cargo ships into lighters, to be towed
to Tate and Lyle's refineries, the sugar in bags till 1949 and
then in bulk, and in October 1962, the Williams Hudson Group
undertook the discharge of Tate and Lyle's largest single
consignment.[10] The Wageners, the Colonel and his wife, and
Varco Williams lie in St. Andrew's churchyard, while Langtons
still stands, the fine house and gardens made over as a gift to
the Hornchurch Council by the Williams family.

Having followed these Victorian refiners to their Essex
homes, their families, and even a tomb, we return to consider
the vanished refineries. Strangely enough, a survivor of the
early sugar house was waiting for me in Essex. The name of
Sugar House Lane at Stratford near the Lea river had always
sounded promising, and I determined to explore, but some
hours of questioning people in that thoroughfare of various
industries revealed ignorance of any sugar house or refinery
ever existing there, till at the premises of Towler and Son, I
was informed that Mr W. Towler, J.P. would have been
interested in my enquiries but was at court that day. Enlisting
the help of the West Ham librarian, Mr. F. Sainsbury, in my
enquiry I informed him of the Towler possibility, whereupon he produced a letter from that Company, in which
among other matters the claim was advanced that their
premises stood on the site of the first sugar refinery in this
country. Interesting as it sounded, we knew it could not be
substantiated, remembering Bussine and his 1544 venture. But
the tradition of a past sugar refinery was evident, and finally

we pin-pointed its site by a Commission of Sewers presentment of 1843, and the West Ham tithes commutation map
of 1853. Here stands a typical gaunt building of the refinery
type, lofty and brick-built, many windowed, overlooking the
Three Mills River, with strong interior walls and arches
corresponding with its outward suggestion. Though the
present occupiers, comparative newcomers, knew nothing of
the building's original purpose, the site, edifice, curve of the
road and its naming, the old family dwelling house at the
factory yard entrance, all supported the presumption that here
was the surviving building of the first refinery in Essex.

As I discovered that the lane was constructed some time
after the refinery, hence the curve of the road around the
premises and its naming, it was not surprising that when the
refinery was described in the 1851 West Ham census returns
the address given was High Road, Stratford, for indeed it is
but a little off the main road. Here was Cord Campe, sugar
refiner from Hanover, Germany, his wife and five children,
and employing two chemists, a sugar baker or panman living
nearby in Union Street, and nine workmen. A trade directory
of the same year (1851) lists only Law Brothers as sugar
refiners at Stratford, so the sugar house apparently changed
owners this year, for directory and census agree in only one
refining business. In the 1861 census no refinery appears.
The 1843 Commission of Sewers presentment mentioned
above gives Elizabeth Reynolds as owner of the sugar
'distillery', meadow, gardens and buildings, and Charles
Saunders as occupier.

The time is near for the first of the huge Silvertown
factories to arise, but one other small Essex business whose
owner is described in the *Trade Directory* as 'sugar refiner'
should be mentioned: Thomas Byham of 29 Long Wyre
Street, Colchester, listed in 1870. Little is known of this
establishment or of him, only that he appears in the
Colchester Poll book for 1870, and that in 1868 his address
was in Military Road.[11] No mention of him or refining appears
in the 1874 directory.

What the conditions were like at this early Stratford refinery

can only be guessed by comparison with an East End refinery
described by an outspoken journalist of 1874,[1][2] who
wrote of such an establishment, under the heading of 'At a
sugar baking'. There is little doubt that journalistic exagger-
ation has made a grim picture worse than reality. He writes
'The innocent-looking sugar lump, so pure, and bright, and
sparkling employs several thousand men in the East End of
London. Around Back Church Lane, Whitechapel, are dozens
of these boiling houses, enormous in size, usually occupying
the whole of a side of a street and very high. A kind-hearted
German missionary acted as guide amid the "sickening reek
of sugar" '. They entered 'a sort of warehouse, dismal, a gas
jet shining foggily, walls steam-coated with black deposit of
sugar and grime, the floor corrugated with the same'.
Gazing up into the 'high blackened roof' he saw 'pendant
from the great supporting bulks of timber were glistening
icicle-shapes and exudings'. On the other side of 'this gloomy
cavern, dimly visible but glowing duskily was a gigantic
globular structure of bright copper, a great pan, all covered
in, in which was gently seething ten tons of liquid sugar, a
small disc of glass in the side showing the bubbling straw-
coloured mass within. The guardian of the pan put in an iron
rod which he called a "key", and pulled it out again with a
little blob of melted sugar, which he took between his
finger and thumb and drew out to a thread by the light of a
gas burner'. From here he was conducted to witness moist
sugar production which was 'in an underground position,
with just enough gas light to show all manner of wriggling
and revolving machinery; our conductor lighted the way with
a torch composed of hastily-twisted newspaper to a vast
underground cellar, lit by an occasional window high up where
the street pavement was. It was very hot, an unctious steam
filling the cellar from end to end, and on one side were two
gigantic pans of sugar, melted hot and smoking, where the
labourers, stripped to waist and sweating, scooped up this
liquor in pails, about ½ cwt., and hurried across the floor
to deposit it in vast revolving basins set in motion at
lightning speed by machinery. The sugar thus dried like

blacklead was shovelled out and taken to the great heap nearly as high as the ceiling. The disgusting conditions brought out a remark from the guide about the workers "They would be dead without their beer unlimited". Through similar scenes our guide conducted us to another sight, the sugar loaf department. On an extensive floor about a hundred feet by seventy feet loaf sugar moulds were packed as closely as the cells of a beehive, placed point downwards into earthen jars for drainage. A dozen semi-naked men were crawling like frogs over the surface of the sugar moulds, getting foot and hand holds on the edges, some with a sort of engine squirting a transparent liquor into the moulds and others stirring the thick stuff in the moulds constantly with their hands. We went up again, to greater heat on crystal-covered stairs, with toffee on hand rails and hard bake on beams to another room full of moulds (12,000 loaves a week are sent from this factory.) The moulds were filled with liquid sugar, that flowed out of great taps — the hardest part of the sugar baking business. The moulds when filled with liquid sugar weigh 1½ cwt., are carried across the great warehouses and arranged close together, each in its own jar, a gang of a dozen men, again stripped to the waist, doing this carrying on piece work, so hurry is the pace. But hurry is not easy with 1½ cwt. of sloppy hot sugar to carry in an inconvenient vessel, and lurches, stumblings, elbowings made the sugar mould hugged to the chest slop over the naked bodies of the carriers, these sloppings harden and crust to a coat inconvenient to wear and disgusting to behold'. Greenlaw goes on to remark that a fair day's work is 12 hours, but can be kept up to 16 or 18 hours without extra pay. Another writer[13] states that at the 'bakers', the refining was carried out by a most primitive process, under conditions so dreadful that even the Rosemary Lane Irish would not tolerate them, and the industry had to be manned by German labour, the cheapest in the whole of the East End. These early refineries were not all so primitive in conditions as that above, we may presume, but these accounts are revealing.

The huge blocks of sugar bakeries, dwarfing the streets of two-storey houses, slowly ceased business and were converted to other purposes (now all vanished, except in Sugar House Lane, Stratford).

Here is a contrasting picture of a sugar refinery through the eyes of a visitor[14] nearly a century later after he had visited Plaistow Wharf. 'A modern sugar refinery is a temple of applied science, operated by skilled technicians rather than manual workers.' To this has the industry advanced from the crude operations of the East End buildings, through the more developed processes housed in those grim piles of Victorian Silvertown, to the modern structures and techniques that succeeded them.

The mention of Dagenham Dock when writing of Varco Williams turns one's thoughts to the Thames, to wonder how many millions of tons of sugar have passed by the Essex shore, along the Thames to London in medieval craft, great sailing ship, or modern vessel, a swelling volume reaching the vast quantity indicated in this report of 1967:[15]

> Total imports = 1,167,000 tons of which 1,100,000 tons were dealt with at riverside premises that are outside the day to day jurisdiction of the Port of London Authority. The remaining 67,000 tons were dealt with in the enclosed docks of the P.L.A. of which 85% was handled at India and Millwall docks, 8% at Tilbury Dock and 7½% at the Royal group of Docks.

Writing about the Thames and sugar leads on to the odd belief held by some people at Plaistow Wharf refinery that Maryland Point, Stratford, in the past had been a lookout position for sugar-laden ships coming up the river to London. Now, it was fairly well known that this district had acquired its name from some fortunate person who had amassed wealth in America and returned here to live, but there seemed no explanation how this tradition of sugar ship observance had arisen, except the very faint possibility that the London refiners residing here could gain by telescope early apprisal of the arrival of a sugar-carrying ship, which knowledge might be of business use.

But the search through local records incidental to the

enquiry did dredge up from the past a bizarre story with a sugar echo. The *Annual Register* for 1865 gave prominence to the account of a murder committed at Silvertown by Ferdinand Kohl, sugar baker (old name for panman). The victim was John Fuhrhop, aged 21, a visitor from Germany and lodging with Kohl. The pronounced German element in the sugar refining world has already been mentioned. At the trial that followed this 'Murder in the Marsh', as the newspapers of the time described it, the evidence included some allusions to early Silvertown and the East End sugar houses. The address of the accused was given as 'Hoy Street, Plaistow Marsh'. This street is still a turning off the Victoria Dock Road, which main road was up to recent years always known to local inhabitants as 'The Marsh', despite the lines of market stalls and shops that afterwards appeared. The money young Fuhrhop was supposed to have brought with him was the motive for his slaying by his host. At that time many solitary stretches of the once great Plaistow Marsh existed in the Silvertown area, and the decapitated body and the head were found in the reeds at such a lonely spot by a man and boy out shooting. A hatchet had been used, and evidently the murderer expected the tide to wash away the body and other traces. On the morning of the day John was last seen, a man employed at the 'Plaistow Wharf' had seen the two together walking on the bank, another saw them near the 'oil works' (this wharf and oil works were to be the site of the future Lyle refiner). Kohl had also been observed returning alone in a muddy condition, others had seen him near the reed bed, and after the coroner's inquest at the *Bell and Anchor* (once near the Victoria Docks) Kohl was arrested on a charge of murder. The accused protested his innocence and stated that on the day in question he and John had journeyed to the East End district, Kohl to seek work again at a sugar house (he had been employed otherwise for a time), his companion to enquire at a London dock for a ship home. They stopped to enable Kohl to enter the 'Iron sugar house' at the upper end of Commercial Road to enquire for work, and when he emerged young Fuhrhop was missing. But the 'porter' at the sugar house denied that Kohl had called there, and with the damning evidence of the bank witnesses the alibi was broken down. Ferdinand Kohl (26) tried desperately to escape the coming retribution, asking for a mixed jury of six English and six foreigners, inducing a brother to swear they were together on the fatal day, and later attempting suicide by thrusting a penholder down his throat. After careful deliberation the jury found him guilty, and he was hanged at Chelmsford Gaol, asserting his innocence to the end. His English wife was exonerated from any participation.

As relief from this gruesome chronicle is a short excerpt from Gilbert's *Bab Ballads*[1 6]

> You do not often get the chance
> Of seeing sugar brokers dance.

Until it was pulled down about 1921, a large rambling farmhouse, reputed to be 300 years old, stood at Plaistow a little south of Barking Road, named Cumberland House, after Henry, Duke of Cumberland, brother of George III, who kept his racing stud there. The 1851 census shows Thomas Fry, sugar broker, here with wife, family and servants. The sugar broker is a most necessary person on the commercial side of the sugar industry, putting into contact the sellers and buyers of sugar quantities. When the old house was demolished, together with an immense tithes barn, the large site was covered with an estate of modest villas (1925) and a group of panmen from the Silvertown refineries became owner-occupiers, because of this the place earning the name of Panville among the Lyle humourists.

Fig. 1. Token of John Parker, Romford, 1669.
Actual size, Diameter 13/16 in.

CHAPTER IV

THE ESSEX ADMIRALS
AND THE SUGAR ISLANDS

THE CARIBBEAN ISLANDS discovered by Christopher Columbus in 1492 were granted to Spain by the Pope. In the course of time the islands were divided between that country, England, and France, with Dutch influence, and the fact that the three Continental nations were like hereditary enemies to England at different times from the Armada to Waterloo meant that in the several wars between these rivals in that period, the West Indies, of tremendous trade value, became a constant cockpit, the islands captured and recaptured in succession. Most of our 18th-century admirals saw service here, in fact, it was the first of the regular sea stations for Britain. The West Indies became the hub of the British Empire, of immense importance to the grandeur and prosperity of England, the most precious colonies ever recorded in the whole annals of imperialism, as many writers have eulogized.

The story of these sugar islands conflicts begins with the first English settlements, the colonists first touching St. Lucia, a longer trial of St. Kitts, then a firm settlement in Barbados in 1641, as already related. This mixture of Puritan England and Catholic Spain was potential for trouble and by Cromwell's time the Spanish harassment of the English settlers, by destruction of property, capture of ships, and enslavement of crews brought the Protector's retaliating attention on the Caribbean scene. He demanded of Spain freedom of trade and complete religious liberty for English colonists, and when the demand was ignored, conceived what was termed the Western Design, the capture and annexation to England of the West Indian islands. To this end in

1654 he dispatched Vice-Admiral William Penn, an experienced seaman, with a fleet of 50 vessels carrying an expedit-
ionary force. Cromwell and Penn are interesting to Essex
people, with sons attending famous schools in the county.
Three of Cromwell's sons, Robert, Oliver and Richard,[1]
attended the Felsted school, a residence in the vicinity,
Grandcourts, belonging to their maternal grandfather Sir
James Bourchier, affording a homelike retreat on days off
and holidays. William, the son of the Admiral, became a
scholar at the Chigwell school.

The fleet departed for the Caribbean adventure in the spring
of 1655, the 2,000 troops under the command of General
Robert Venables with orders to recruit more among the
colonists. First Barbados, then the Leeward Islands were taken,
and in April Penn sailed in for Cromwell's chief objective,
Hispaniola (now Haiti, and the Dominican Republic). The
force attacked the city of Santa Domingo but were repulsed,
the overland march tiring the troops who in any case were
of poor quality, with disease and bad water thinning their
numbers, so that Penn withdrew to sea with the dispirited
survivors. The expedition had failed in the main assault and
Penn rather than return almost empty-handed to the vengeful
Protector sailed on and captured Jamaica on 10 May. This
was not enough, and on returning to England Penn and
Venables were condemned to the Tower by the disappointed
Cromwell. There were charges of cowardice and perhaps dis-
affection, Penn being not without some royalist leanings.

Before following Penn's emergence from his disgrace, two
aspects of this Caribeean episode are considered. Despite
Cromwell's disappointment the expedition has an important
place in the foundation of the Navy, and in providing another
of those overseas bases without which command of the sea
cannot be maintained. And during the activities in Hispaniola
a well known Essex name is seen again, Francis Barrington;[2]
he had served as captain of a troop in Colonel Okey's
dragoons, and in 1649-50 was in a new regiment of horse
for action in Ireland. In the Hispaniola attack, the dis-
embarking regiment was under the command of Colonel

Buller, with Lieutenant-Colonel Barrington second-in-command. Buller's directions were to land and attack east of the river Jayna, but circumstances forced him to land west of that objective, and the failure to carry out the original order prematurely revealed to the enemy the plan of campaign that Venables intended to follow, so that the General laid the blame of unsuccess on the Colonel. Barrington strongly criticised Venables in letters written after the event for not taking officers into his confidence, and upheld Buller. Later, after the occupation of Jamaica, he did good work in land cultivation and stock-raising and in combating marauding negro slaves left behind by the Spaniards. In 1657 Colonel Doyley, commander-in-chief of the Jamaican forces, when applying for leave to visit England recommended Barrington as the one to take his place, inasmuch that he was a kinsman of the Protector and 'a man of known integrity, competent abilities', and with his experience and willingness to stay in the island had 'genius much inclined to the way of plantation'. It was the colony's loss that in 1660 he was killed by an accident.

The stay of Penn and Venables in the Tower was short, and no doubt a time of reflection, as it was alleged that quarrels between the two men during the Hispaniola expedition had helped its failure. Later Penn entered into the growing Royalist cause, and at the Restoration was knighted.

While still in his 40s, he purchased a house at Wanstead,[3] and after his death here his widow continued residence for some years, the famed Chigwell school four miles away receiving the Admiral's son William as a pupil. But Sir William knew Essex long before residing there. He served as commissioner on the Navy Board, of which Samuel Pepys the diarist was Secretary, and the Diary has some lively accounts of the two men travelling from London by horse or carriage to the Walthamstow house of another Commissioner, Sir W. Batten. Despite the surface friendship of Pepys and Penn, the diarist made some scurrilous comments on Penn's character and ability, but the verdict of history on this Admiral and General-at-Sea is that he was a capable commander, and much commended by the Duke of York (the future James II) who as High Admiral of the Fleet would be better placed to pass judgment than the jaundiced Pepys.

An Essex interest lies in the fact that the Cromwell design to annex the Spanish West Indies was revived not many years after in which scheme participated Daniel Defoe, of 'Robinson Crusoe' fame, who in his life and writings established several connections with our county. (See chapter 6). As William III prepared for the great struggle in Europe which would arise from the contending claimants to the Spanish crown and the power it would give on the Continent, Defoe strongly supported and urged an alternative to the coming blood-bath in the European cockpit, a war on the sea and the capture of the Spanish colonies in the Caribbean. He prepared designs for plans of attack on the islands, and submitted them to the king, who had the scheme under consideration, but it was finally shelved in 1703.

Though disappointed at what he regarded as Penn's failure Cromwell began to colonise the new acquisition, and made 'Proclamation to such as transplant themselves to Jamaica, of grants of land, rights of fishing, discovered minerals, and other benefits', and among those who sought new life here were Scotsmen, 1,000 Irish girls, and others who freely or perforce wanted to leave England. The plantations of sugar cane, gradually increasing over other crops, needed a large labour force, and this, plus the failure of some white workers to adapt themselves to climate and work conditions, led to Jamaica following the Spanish and Portuguese examples, and introducing negro slave labour, which innovation and its gigantic growth with Essex participation in the two and a half centuries to come, are left to another chapter.

As the colony became integrated an administrative body was created, consisting of a Legislature drawn from the planters and wealthy merchants, under a Governor appointed from Britain by the Crown, and Essex has a representative among these royal appointments, if not an admiral, yet the son of one. Among the many titles bestowed on George

Monck for his great share in the Restoration by a grateful Charles II was Duke of Albemarle and, more interesting to us, Admiral of the Navy. As such in 1664 he won an important victory over the Dutch. In 1668 he retired to New Hall, an imposing Tudor building with a royal history in the parish of Boreham. When he died in 1670 the dukedom passed to his son Christopher,[4] who created an Essex-Jamaica link.

Royal visits to New Hall, the functions of Court, the coronation of James II in which the new duke carried the sceptre and dove, the ceremonies of his office as joint Lord-Lieutenant of Essex were against a background of extravagant living which depleted his large fortune, necessitating sale of some of his extensive property. Some lack of success in his campaign against the Monmouth rebellion in 1685 caused the King to supplant him in command by Lord Faversham, and this waning of royal favour, his diminished resources, and ill-health brought him to broody seclusion at New Hall. However, at the age of 34 life is far from over, and he turned to a novel and romantic way of renewing the family fortune. Before the King's loss of confidence in him the Duke had obtained royal assent to a claim on a distant hidden treasure in the Caribbean area, a sunken Spanish galleon laden with valuable cargo including precious metals, a victim of the many hazards incurred by a rich ship coming from the Spanish Main. Here was golden opportunity and with a company named the Merchant Adventurers the treasure was recovered in 1687, Albemarle receiving as his share £90,000. Eager to continue the operations after such a fabulous windfall, and to gain a favourable position, he applied for and was given the post of Governor of Jamaica, and he and the Duchess arrived there in December 1687. Almost before settling into the Governor's chair he organised successful recoveries of other sunken treasurers, the gold and silver ingots representing enormous value. Some wish fulfilments exact high payment, and Albemarle was dead within the year, his health collapsing in the Jamaican climate and conditions. The corpse, preserved in coffin and pitch, was brought home for burial in Westminster Abbey.

A few years after, a naval celebrity in Caribbean conflicts to have links with Essex was that colourful character Vice-Admiral John Benbow.[5] At a time when officers of the Navy were drawn from the upper classes and resentful of any intrusion from below into their preserve, John Benbow, of humble origin, graduated from the lower deck to command over officers who disdained him as a 'tarpaulin', a term of contempt for those few of their members of lowly birth. Benbow is said to be a saddler's son, was apprenticed to a butcher, and afterwerds ran off to sea where energetic qualities and natural aptitude for seamanship brought him promotion from below to the quarterdeck. As a young officer he served with distinction against the Algerian pirates and became a brilliant commander; temper and tact, however, suffered from his knowledge of the lack of respect for him by his officers, his resentment of this widening the breach between them, leading to tragic results. Knowing the circumstances of his birth, there seems no difficulty in believing the assertion that he had some residence at Plaistow, Essex. We owe this knowledge to John James, bailiff of West Ham Manor in 1742, who wrote *A survey of Plaistow,* describing all houses and cottages. He gives particulars of two neighbouring houses, one owned by Mr. Richard Pennock, the other tenanted by Mr. James Benbow, and from this has come down the belief that Admiral Benbow once lived in the latter house. J.S. Curwen in *Old Plaistow* passes on this tradition (but states he was unable to obtain verification) and shows a sketch of a wooden house with overhanging storey at Pinnocks Place, the reputed home; a photograph of this is exhibited at the Passmore Edwards Museum, Stratford. The house was pulled down in 1905 and Pinnocks Place, opposite St. Mary's Church, has itself disappeared since. The story of Benbow's last battle in 1702 reveals class distinctions operating even at the cannon's mouth. He had been created rear-admiral in 1696, later appointed Commander-in-Chief of the West Indies region. In the War of the Spanish Succession between England and the Netherlands against France, the conflict inevitably spilled over into the Carribbean Sea, and an elusive French commander, du Casse, who was spreading havoc around the sugar islands, was at length brought to battle by Benbow off Santa Marta, but his captains refused to follow Benbow into action on the grounds that they had only seven ships to the enemy's 10 (although four of the French ships were small). Seeing his prey escaping, he attacked with only three vessels, which in this one-sided fight received a battering, yet despite this and a wound that cost him a leg, as Du Casse withdrew Benbow would have pursued him, but still his captains refused to follow their despised leader. Afterwards, the offenders were brought to trial and two shot on the charge of cowardice.

The next admiral in time who I thought might have an Essex connection was Admiral Vernon, a surmise prompted by a prominent public house named after him and displaying a reproduction of his portrait by Gainsborough, in the market thoroughfare of Broad Street, Dagenham. However, there was no historical connection with this borough or the county, but it was surprising to learn that the owning brewers, Courage Ltd. did not know why this house was so named, their records not extending back to when the tavern was built, 1939. The date made it obvious to me, the bicentenary year of Vernon's naval exploit which made him a national hero and a name for many pubs and inns. During hostilities in the Caribbean between British and Spanish arising from opposed trading rights, feeling in this country was strongly intensified by Spanish captors cutting off the ear of a marauding Welsh captain named Jenkins. Amid the clamour for war over this and other indignities, a certain Captain Edward Vernon publicly declared that with six ships he would capture the important Spanish base of Portobello on the Panama Isthmus, and so singe the Spaniard's beard. This he did, to the great joy of the English people at home. The people at the Dagenham *Admiral Vernon* knew nothing of this, but characteristically knew that Vernon introduced 'grog' into the Navy.

In 1751 another admiral had a faint Essex-sugar echo, Charles Knowles, Governor of Jamaica,[6] who attempted to change the capital of the island from Spanish Town to Kingston. His action aroused strong resentment, a model of his ship the *Cornwall* publicly burnt, so that the scheme after much ado was abandoned (the change was made in 1871). In accordance with the Navy custom of perpetuating the names of ships the Knowles *Cornwall*, after finishing her West Indian career and broken up in 1761, was succeeded by another of that name[7] which also served in the Caribbean till badly damaged in 1780 at the battle of St. Lucia (in which engagement another Essex admiral took part, who will be considered later). The battle-seared vessel, her fighting days ended, was followed in 1812 by another *Cornwall* which after nearly 50 years of sea service became a reformatory vessel of the School Ship Society in 1859, moored off Purfleet for nine years and devoted to the care of friendless boys. She was then moved to South Shields for similar service, her place in the Thames taken by H.M.S. *Wellesley*, a former East India Company ship of 1815, 74 guns, and as the ships changed names, again a T.S. *Cornwall* was seen off Purfleet, till recent years.

In 1759, 'the year of victories', Admiral Moore and General John Barrington captured from the French the island of Guadeloupe, and the second name emerges into the Essex admirals later. When England suffered the reverses in the American War of Independence in 1777, our old enemies Spain, France, Holland, seized the chance of annexing our West Indian possessions and de Bouille, Governor of French Martinique, began a plan of conquest by taking Dominica. He prepared for further annexations in 1778, but was thwarted by the swift action and the clever capture of St. Lucia island by an admiral of Essex origin, Samuel Barrington, who was the fifth son of Viscount (John) Barrington of Tofts in Essex.

'Unfortunately for the British' as one historian phrases it,[8] after St. Lucia Barrington was replaced by a senior officer, Admiral Byron, whose conduct of the campaign left the Caribbean in a perilous position till the famed Admiral Rodney defeated the French fleet at the Battle of the Saintes in 1782. Political strife at home could affect the Navy in these times, and some officers declined to serve under such infiltration. Barrington consented to act as the second-in-command only, and the intrigues created the dangerous position of 'our four best officers' Rodney, Keppel, Howe and Barrington held idle while events at sea were growing disastrous. However, the political atmosphere cleared later, and the *London Gazette* of 1788 informs us of the promotion of the Hon. Samuel Barrington to Admiral of the Blue. He died in 1800.

The same number of the *London Gazette* has the notice of promotion of Sir John Jervis, K.B., our next Essex worthy, to Rear-Admiral of the Blue. In Stuart times, red, white and blue flags distinguished the three naval squadrons in rank of sailing order, red in the van, and later this was formalised as a scale of promotion for officers, first the three squadron admirals in order of colour, then the vice-admirals, followed by the rear-admirals.

Thus the 1788 posting shows John Jervis (now Sir John) the celebrated Essex admiral, commencing his ascent of the higher naval hierarchy, the admirals or 'flagmen'; a long ladder of seniority, for even the great Nelson at his death was but Rear-Admiral of the White. Jervis resided at a house named Rochetts at South Weald, and his connection with the West Indies was both naval and financial. Of him it has been written 'he was unquestionably one of the greatest naval officers that Britain ever produced, at once fighter, strategist, leader and administrator. More than any other officer, by his perception, encouragement, and kindness, he moulded the character and ensured the future of the greatest officer of all', Nelson, who served under Jervis. With a record of re-sounding successes, Sir John was created Earl St. Vincent and later was called to Whitehall as First Lord of the Admiralty.

He drew an income from West Indian sugar plantations. When in 1837 the negro slaves who worked on them were emancipated, and the British Government paid compensation to owners dispossessed of their human property, the Earl had died, and his heir Viscount St. Vincent received £6,000 for his 418 slaves, according to one writer.[9] Examination of B.M. records lists Viscount St. Vincent and Vere Fare with £4,442 for 218 slaves, and the Viscount with Sir William

Parker and Frances Beckford £1,746 for share in 200 slaves.[10]
The Admiral had something of the toughness of the oak of
his ships in his own mental build. He pleaded the plantations
were a paradise for the negro compared with his native
Africa, and was of the opinion that abolition of Slavery was
'a damned and cursed doctrine, held only by hypocrites', a
fulmination probably sincerely felt but perhaps affected to
some extent by his pocket. In fairness to the Earl it should
be stated that he was far from alone in this support of slavery.
Lord Nelson held forth: 'I was taught to appreciate the value
of our West Indian possessions . . . and while I have an arm
to fight in their defence, or a tongue to launch my voice
against Wilberforce and his damnable opinions . . . their just
rights will not be infringed'. He also claimed the slave trade
bred good sailors for the Navy!

The Earl appears something of a despot in parish records
but a good benefactor to the poeple.[11] Set on high ground
with fine views of surrounding country, still stands the house
'Rochetts' where he resided. A wing was built on his orders
in six months, and the lake below with its water lilies is also
his work. The small hamlet nearby named St. Vincent recalls
his day of triumph in a very different setting in 1797.

Among the Essex naval officers who served in the West
Indies was Eliab (later Sir Eliab) Harvey, born at Hempstead[12]
in 1758, a descendant of the famous William Harvey who was
discoverer of the circulation of the blood (burier at Hempstead). Eliab entered the Navy as 'middy' at the tender age of
11, and by 1793 was captain of a frigate at the West Indian
station. War between England and France at this time meant
careful guarding of the sugar islands, of fabulous wealth and
tempting prizes for the enemy. Before the peace of 1801
the captain had been transferred to the Channel fleet, so that
after he had served as M.P. for Essex during the peace, the
resumption of the war in 1803 brought him the command of
the *Temeraire,* the ship immortalised by Turner's famous
painting, and this was the vessel Captain Harvey brought into
the Battle of Trafalgar, 1805. 'No admiral had ever had better
support than Nelson from Captain Harvey, a bold gambler, a

man of outspoken temper and a doughty fighter.' Later Harvey served as Rear-Admiral under Lord St. Vincent and was promoted to full Admiral in 1819. He died in 1830 and was buried at St. Andrew's, Hempstead.

At Trafalgar in the line of battle headed by the flagship *Victory*, followed by the *Temeraire*, was the *Conqueror*, on board of which was a young midshipman, William Hicks, destined to be vicar of an Essex parish, Sturmer, for 44 years.

The great Nelson himself, who has a small niche in Essex, saw much service in the West Indies and found a wife in the island of Nevis. A look-out point at Fort Charles, Jamaica, where he long kept watch for a hostile French fleet, is known as 'Nelson's Quarterdeck', and on the wall is a tablet:[13]

In this place dwelt Horatio Nelson
You who tread his footprints,
Remember his glory

His chaplain and secretary, almost personal friend, was the Revd. Alexander Scott, and who on the *Victory* administered to the dying Admiral. Scott's devotion to Nelson was deep, he remained night and day at the lying in state in the Painted Hall, Greenwich, and after leaving the sea and becoming vicar of Southminster, Essex, he brought with him and gave to the church, St. Leonard's, the mementos from the *Victory*, which are a large chart table (on which today's wedded couples sign the register), a bureau, mirror, and firegrate, bringing into the quiet vestry memories of past stirring times. It has been claimed, and upheld by descendants of the Revd. Scott who visit the relics at intervals,[14] that Nelson himself used these articles, the reason for their preservation by his devoted chaplain and friend.

A brief note concerning the Army's Essex and West Indies connections. During the war with France that started in 1793, the 44th Foot (East Essex Regiment) and the 56th Foot (West Sussex Regiment, the Pompadours) were engaged in the capture of the islands of Martinique, Guadeloupe, and St. Lucia.

CHAPTER V

ESSEX AND THE SUGAR SLAVES

BEHIND the increasing production of sugar in the islands of the Caribbean and its increasing use and enjoyment in all classes, behind the huge fortunes and aristocratic assumptions of the plantation owners, the gallant exploits of the admirals in capture of defence of the sugar islands, lay the sombre shadow of negro slavery, the forced impounding, the sale and purchase, the lifelong subjugation to toil and master of millions of African natives, lasting nearly three centuries. Even the children born of them became the property of the master; a gigantic enslavement of mankind that built up the empire of sugar. It has been estimated that in the 300 years of New World slavery, nearly 20 million negroes were removed from Africa, the larger portion destined for the sugar plantations. Spain and Portugal introduced the captive black slave to the sugar plantation, and as the demand for such labour increased, the business of supplying the required slaves became as lucrative as plantation owning. Before England moved into the Caribbean islands as sugar producers she had engaged in the slave trade through John Hawkins and Francis Drake, whose slave ships operated under the aegis of Elizabeth I; her expressed disapproval of the sorry business did not render her adverse to its profitable side. An Essex participator in this slave trade was Thomas Lodge[1] who described himself as 'of West Ham', a City merchant engaged in foreign trade, and in 1559 was Master of the Grocers' Company. He at times financed ships to explore the North African coasts for possible markets, and as a variation about 1562 he and other citizens obtained a charter from the Queen for two ships, the *Mynyon* and the *Prymrose* to operate in the ports of Africa and Ethiopia. 'To this voyage has been

assigned the unenviable distinction of inaugurating the in-
famous traffic in negro slaves.'[2] Another transaction by Lodge
was with others to provide money for Sir John Hawkins to fit
out three ships for trading in slaves taken from Guinea, which
earned such good profits that a similar venture was backed
the following year, 1563. It was during this slavery business
that Lodge was made Lord Mayor of London. He possessed
property in West Ham and London, also owned the manor of
Malmaynes in Barking, and at his death in 1584 left a £5
bequest to the poor of West Ham. He was the father of Thomas
Lodge, poet and pamphleteer, who was associated with West
Ham and Leyton and who is credited with some collaboration
with Shakespeare in *As you like it.*

Because of growing demand for sugar and the greater
number of plantations with need for more labourers, the
supply of negro slaves became increasingly profitable, the
ships of Bristol, London, and Liverpool carrying goods to
Africa to barter for slaves, with the gained cargo of negroes
continuing the journey to the West Indies, then with the
proceeds of the human sale stocking with sugar, rum and other
Caribbean products to take back to England, the whole trip
known as the Triangular Passage. In 1672 the Royal African
Company was chartered with Charles and his queen leading
the list of subscribers, giving its members the monopoly of
the growing English slave trade on the African coast, and at
Guinea forts were erected to guard dealer and booty from
pirate raids and other hazards. A greater impetus to trade
came by gaining a further monopoly, the Asiento, which was
a contract rented out by Spain for the supply of 4,800 slaves
a year to her New World colonies, held first by the Dutch,
then the French, and then, as one of the agreements in
the Treaty of Utrecht in 1713, accorded to Britain. With this
and the monopolies already owned, the Royal African
Company put England beyond European rivals in this business,
for by the middle of the 18th century her traders were
shipping negroes from Africa at the rate of 40,000 annually,
mostly for sugar.[3] Much of the loading of slaves was on the
African coast of Guinea, which gave its name to a new coin

put into the British currency, first made of Guinea gold.

Among the directors of the Royal African Company could be found in 1730 an unexpected Essex name, James Olgethorpe, surprising when one considers his later great and deserved reputation as promoter of one of the greatest humanitarian projects, the founding of the American colony of Georgie for the reception and settlement of the impoverished and hopeless victims of debtors' prisons. In view of his previous activity some change of heart is indicated, for he steadfastly refused to admit slaves and rum into the new colony. General James Oglethorpe is buried in Cranham church, near which he resided in later life.

Another Essex man, from Plaistow, with a finger in this dubious pie was John Atkins, a naval surgeon and author of travel and medical books. In a work of 1735 he describes his participation in the slaving business[4] as incidental to his position of surgeon in the Navy. The Royal African Company, with which so many influential and high-ranking people were connected, experienced much trouble from the depredations of pirates and loss of trade by interlopers, and vessels from the Navy were assigned for protection. Whether the Company's vessels were proceeding to Guinea laden with textiles, hardware, guns, powder, cutlasses, liquor, toys, beads, trinkets to barter for slaves with the supplying African chiefs, whether bound for the New World packed with slaves, or whether returning to England with sugar and other plantation produce, they were a worthwhile prize for the many pirate captains, who had a 'black market' rendezvous of their own. One marauder named Roberts had become a scourge to the 'legitimate' trade, capturing 400 prizes, burning many of the slave ships after removing the valuable living cargo, attacking and looting the Guinea shore ports. In 1722 the Navy sent two frigates after him, the *Swallow* and *Weymouth*, Atkins serving as surgeon. After a long pursuit from Sierra Leone along the slave coast to Whydah, H.M.S. *Swallow* eventually discovered Roberts's ship, the *Royal Fortune*, anchored in a vulnerable spot on the Guinea coast, and when the pirate attempted to escape by putting out to sea a broadside from the frigate killed Roberts and brought surrender of the marauder ship. The crew of 52 were hanged on the beach.

It appeared that naval vessels protecting the chartered slavers engaged themselves a little in the business, carrying a cargo of commodities that could be bartered for slaves, the ship's captain sometimes undertaking the duty of super-cargo or agent; in Atkins's case, it was the surgeon, for he added to his medical activities that of supercargo. He learnt that for the black chiefs who supplied the slaves, and for the white dealers, the best articles for barter were firearms, cutlasses, and liquor, while a full Guinea cargo for slave exchange would include cottons and silks, sheets, kettles, pans and scales, tankards and knives, beads and other gew-gaws. The slaves supplied by the African chiefs (so there were both black and white participators in the trade) were the criminals and offenders against the multiple tribal laws and customs, supplemented by the prisoners-of-war, victims of native warfare sometimes fomented to gain prisoners. Chiefs would sell their own people village by village. Kidnapping parties, white and black, would raid the interior and the long line or 'coffle' of captives, the men fastened to a long chain or linked together in batches, marched down to the coast past the burnt villages, the whips of the drivers curling around the slow or reluctant. Some native families were forced by poverty to sell some of their own people. Despite his fin-ancial interest in slavery, Atkins was not without consider-ation for the wretched plight of these victims. He observes the chaining in threes and fours while awaiting sale at Whydah and the naked condition of men and women, their sole garment, the loincloth, stolen from them by the Whydah natives. He rejected the stock arguments by the interested that as slaves these people would be better off than in hazards of jungle and primitive life; with no rights, not even in wife and children, in subjection to exploiting owners, they would be less damned and degraded, he considered, left in their native settlements in spite of brown bread and the Christian doctrine. He writes about the manatee or sea-cow, and how its inch-thick skin can be made into a cruelly cutting strap for punishing refractory slaves in the West Indies. At Whydah a slave physically satisfactory will fetch £15, he observes, and then writes unfavourably of the white traders and factors, their deterioration in habits. The 'General' of the district and his negro mistress and four children were attended medically by Atkins, who notes how the big fellow dotes on her, wants her to journey to England with him, but the woman refuses and persists in her native dress with the customary bangles on arms and feet and in the ears.

John Atkins in his book describes himself as a 'Gentleman of Plaistow, Essex'. The Georgian survey of Plaistow prepared by John James, already mentioned in connection with Admiral Benbow, describes a house owned and resided in by Mr. John Atkins, catalogued as 'modern', brick built in 1712 by a Josiah Phipps. Also mentioned is 'A little boarded house built by the said John Atkins about 1728' of two upper chambers and two lower. In addition to the book already mentioned, Atkins published some medical works; a copy of one is inscribed 'To Yale College, from the author, Plaistow, the 25th February, 1728/9'. This presentation was through Jeremiah Dummer,[5] an American (born 1681) who acted as Colonial Agent in London for Connecticut, residing in later years at Plaistow and an assiduous collector of books for the Yale College (later University).

The ending of the Asiento, and of the Royal African Company in 1750 left the sphere of slave trading open to all, which helped to build up a sugar enslavement unique in the history of slavery, because of its extent and duration. Much literature exists concerning the slave trade, and the worst tales are those told of that part of the triangular sea route followed by the slavers known as the Middle Passage, the journey from Africa to the Caribbean islands, with a packed cargo of black slaves. Unhygienic wooden vessels, the holds filled to capacity or more, a breeding ground for dysentery, ophthalmic and other diseases, these conditions meant it was usual for a percentage to die and be thrown overboard. To reach port after a journey lasting from a month to two months according to weather without loss of human cargo was so exceptional that it called for some celebration, which introduces us to John Newton, religious slaver, a boyhood in Essex, who held a service of thanksgiving when reaching Jamaica without loss of negro, achieving this because he was a humane captain.

John Newton[6] (1725-1807) the hymn writer and divine, the friend of Cowper, was born in London, son of a captain in the Mediterranean trade. As with many famous men, his mother was of religious life, but she died when he was aged six. Two years later John was taken by his father to the Essex village of Aveley and introduced to the house of a prosperous grocer, from whose family came the lady to be the captain's second wife. Soon after the wedding, the boy now 11, was sent to a boarding school at Stratford. He had received some education from his mother and could read at four years, but his time at this school was unhappy and of little mental profit, and the belief of the master in hardening conditions and strict discipline, his savage severity 'almost broke my spirit and my relish for books. Forgotten were the principles of arithmetic my mother taught me'. Occasionally during holidays he went home to Aveley, then a typical Essex village, and though his welcome there was less loving than his mother's and the new step-brother engaging the household, it was a relief from school, though he was left much to himself, to wander about the village and find what company he could among the local boys. His second year at the school was more propitious for he had learned Latin before he was 10 and now could read Tully and Virgil. Then followed a year at Aveley of idleness with occasional consorting with village boys, but making one gain of lasting value, love of the Essex countryside, and perhaps in these young ramblings the differing influences of a dissenting mother and of a father educated in a Jesuit college in Seville may have blended to produce the fertile soil which pushed a rare blossom through the unlikely layers of the years that followed.

When a little older he was taken aboard his father's ship in Long Reach, and commenced his several voyages in the Mediterranean trade, spending shore leave at Aveley. Through

missing the boat after all arrangements were made John failed
to take up a position as trainee manager of a Jamaica sugar
estate, and in a period of idleness which followed tripped
over a strange Essex link, for in 1741 while near the river
in London he was captured by a press gang and put on board
H.M.S. *Harwich*, built at and named after the Essex port.
His father as member of the Royal African Company
obtained his son's release. A childhood memory of John's
was seeing on a wharf near the Tower a heap of metal collars,
chains, and 'mouth-openers' for those persistently refusing
food, which he was told were for West Indian slaves, and
closer acquaintance with such objects was to be his, for he
accepted command of a slave ship owned by a Liverpool
friend of his father. In common with the age, he felt no
compunction in engaging in slaving; did not the Bible support
this condition of man, which also dated back to antiquity!
Even the experience of religious conversion during a storm
made no change in the slave trade attitude. The newly-
wakened spiritual feeling found expression in hymn-writing,
and it is believed that while awaiting a 'coffle' or convoy of
gathered slaves to take on board he composed the words of
the famous hymn beginning:

> How sweet the name of Jesus sounds
> In a believer's ear.

But he came to realise the horror of the slaver's business, and
to write 'I know of no method of getting money, not even
that of robbing for it upon the highway, which has so direct
a tendency to efface the moral sense, to rob the heart of
every gentle and humane disposition, and to harden it like
steel against impressions of sensibility'. The burden of guilt
for a business at which 'My heart shudders' was less heavy
than that which lay upon other slave-captains, for he
treated his living cargo with humanity and consideration.
His awakening to the viciousness of the slaving business,
and its abjuraton, led him later into ordination, becoming
rector of St. Mary Woolnoth, Lombard Street, and the
author of many hymns. In 1788 he aided Wilberforce in the
movement for abolition of slavery by publishing his own

1. The Hon. Samuel Barrington. From an original oil painting by Sir Joshua Reynolds, 1779. By courtesy of the National Maritime Museum. See Chapter 4.

The French Fleet attacking the English Fleet in St. Lucia Bay, 15th December '78. By courtesy of the National Maritime Museum. See Chapter 4.

3. The Old Refinery, Sugar House Lane, Stratford. See Chapter 3.

4. Bee Boles, Eastbury House, Barking. See Chapter 1.

5. *'Forecaster', Beet-harvester.* **See Chapter 9.**

6. *Outpost of Bee Farm, centred at Mayland.* **See Chapter 1.**

7. *Beet Factory, Felsted.* See Chapter 9.

8. *The Tate Gallery.* By courtesy of *The Tate Gallery, London.* See Chapter 4.

experiences of the slave trade 'a temperate, restrained, but ghastly recital of facts'. A fantastic tale of a brand from the burning and Essex is credited with some formative years. In that imposing London church his pulpit still stands.

As contrast to Newton's safe landing with complete living cargo are grim records of Liverpool, which town in the 18th century succeeded London and Bristol as England's greatest slave port, and connects with our Essex sugar story through Tate and Lyle. Oft told is the tale of the 18th-century actor, George Cooke,[7] who appeared on the stage of the Theatre Royal, Liverpool, obviously in a state of intoxication, and was booed by the audience, whereupon from the footlights he shouted back, 'I have not come here to be insulted by a set of wretches, every inch in whose infernal town is cemented with an African's blood'. Was this only drunken nonsense, or a case of 'in vino veritas', truth with the wine? Indeed, the city gained much of its early growth and prosperity from the slave trade, while the articles taken for slave barter helped other manufacturing towns.

Clarkson, the abolitionist, made a count of 20 voyages which together conveyed 7,904 slaves at commencement of the Middle Passage of which 2,053 died before the voyages were completed. The conditions of the journey were such that deaths were regarded as inevitable despite the value of slaves.

Among other reputed Essex slavers is the mariner Captain Samuel Bonham,[8] a successful trader, of whom there is a tradition that slaves were sometimes the cargo. In 1740, when he was 63, he built in Orsett a fine red-brick mansion named Orsett House, which still stands, approached by chestnut avenue and with 13 acres of meadow and parkland. He was buried in 1745 in the churchyard vault surmounted by a lofty stone monument.

In the Essex Record Office is a notebook[9] belonging to John Redman who was in the 18th century at Tyler Halls Farm, Upminster. Among the accounts, building instructions, measurements, medical recipes, descriptions of repairs, complaints, farm records and memoranda, wills, items of general knowledge, occurs the note: 'My grandfather Branfill's name was Andrew, was born in the West Country at Dartmouth, was Captain of a Guinea Man'. This revealing entry is of the Andrew Branfill who in 1685 purchased the manor of Upminster Hall as an investment, his professional activities making Stepney a more convenient place to reside, and not till four generations after did the family fully occupy the Hall. Captain of a guineaman when he was 19 (1659) in the early days of slaving, he later possessed his own ship, *The Champion*. He named his eldest son after it, the name passed on to the eldest son of each generation afterwards.[10] Thus a Champion Branfill entered into Upminster Hall as residence. With its 15th-century hall, it has served as the headquarters of the Upminster Golf Club since 1927.

Mention of Upminster introduces the subject of the owners of slave-worked sugar plantations. Sir James Esdaile (died 1793) was lord of the manor of Gaynes, Upminster. and built several of the former large residences which gave distinction to the parish, Harwood Hall (1782) a remaining example. He was knighted in 1766, while sheriff of London and Middlesex, and possessed a town house in Bunhill Row. That he was part owner of a Jamaican sugar estate known as the Rose Hill Plantation comes from the records of Davison, Newman and Co.,[11] in Creechurch Lane who shared ownership with him and others. The slave muster-book still exists, which records that in 1784 the slave labour force was 220 men, women, boys and girls. Among the juveniles, two aged six were employed in weeding canes. (English pauper children earlier in the century were apprenticed when seven.) Among the more odd names of these slaves were Neptune, Venus, Jupiter, Hannibal, Suckey (a washerwoman) and Ebony. Marlborough (29) a field worker, was 'a noted runaway'. The cane crop varied, 166 hogsheads (or tons) of sugar in 1832, only 82 in 1835, the sugar selling around 58s. per cwt. from which a 27s. duty had to be deducted. Rose Hill Estate survived the difficulties following emancipation and still exists (1938).

Among other Essex owners of slave-worked sugar plantations in the West Indies was a family group descending from the Hon. William Mathew, Governor of the Leeward Islands,[12] a British colony comprising several islands, chief among which were Antigua, St. Kitts, Nevis, Anguilla, Montserrat. In 1752 he devised to his grandson William Mathew of Great Baddow his plantations in Antigua and St. Kitts (shortened from St. Christopher). In 1761 William covenants with Daniel Mathew to hold Drewshill plantation in Antigua for 25 years at £500 per annum, and an appraisement of this large plantation includes a schedule of 100 slaves, their age, condition, worth, how employed, and a report on the quality of the sugar cane. In the marriage settlement of William Mathew and Juliana Brogrove are mentioned West Indian plantations, sugar and rum works, slaves, with an Essex conjunction of properties in Tillingham, Dengie, and High Hall, Walthamstow.

On the death of William in 1764, his only child Juliana inherited the considerable estates on both islands, and by her marriage in 1773 to John Conyers of Copped Hall, Epping, another county name comes into West Indian owner-ship. (Gerald Conyers, knight and alderman, is somewhere on the family roll of that century.) Previous to the marriage had occurred some Chancery suits in the family, in one of which the point at issue linked Felix Hall, Kelvedon, with a West Indian plantation, another concerned the holding of land called Cockenholes of the manor of Epping Bury as security for the value of negroes on Drewshill Plantation in Antigua. Both Mathew and Conyers were 'absentee owners', leaving the care of their sugar estates to managers or overseers and reports and correspondence from the islands to Essex indicate the intermittent hazards in the Caribbean areas. Hurricanes could inflict enormous damage, and a 1772 report described destruction on the Drewshill Plantation — a ruinous dwelling house, half the 51 slaves of no value. An overthrow of a different kind came from the international situation. Following the several reverses of the British in the war against the American colonists the ancient enemies, Spain, France, and Holland joined in the attack on the wounded

Lion, the conflict inevitably embracing the prized West Indian
sugar islands. The French admiral, du Grasse, as part of a
general conquest of the West Indies, landed a strong force on
St. Kitts in February 1782. The colonists retreated to the hilly
interior from where the French troops were unable to drive
them, and a letter from Thomas Stedman to John Conyers
enumerates the calamities to the plantations attending the
siege, the crops gone, the negroes absconded, a camp on the
plantation, also mentioning the disappointment of the
inhabitants over the lack of any counter action by the British
troops in St. Lucia. Surrender was but a matter of time unless
some intervention came, and Admiral Hood sailed down from
the American war area to relieve the island, but though by
good manoeuvering he was able to get between the French
fleet and the island, the French land force was too strong
for him, the British colonists surrendered on 13 February and
the island became French property. The victorious du Grasse
sailed off for his next conquest, Jamaica. But a greater sailor
than Hood was on the way, Admiral Rodney, who, as
described in Chapter IV, brought du Grasse to battle near the
group of little islands known as the Saintes and defeated the
Frenchman. St. Kitts by treaty was restored to Britain. A
third threat was added to those of tempest and war, crippling
taxation, as witnessed in an Antigua letter from James Gordon
to Copped Hall advising Conyers to sell his negroes in Antigua
or evacuate them to St. Kitts, because of a tax imposed by
the Antiguan Assembly on absentee proprietors. The letter
stated 'The tax will fall heavy on proprietors who are
absent, £60 on every 30 negroes unless you keep a white
overseer for every 30. I am in hopes that the Council will
reject the Act, but first it will be incumbent upon the
proprietors who live in England to have it rejected by the
King'. The Assembly, the governing body below the Council,
claimed the tax was necessary to meet 'current expenses'.
A curious complication for Conyers was the objection of
Thomas Brogrove, a relative on his wife's side, that the
removal of negroes to St. Kitts would be a breach of the marriage settlement. How all this was resolved is yet to be
discovered.

The Tyrell family is a notable one in Essex and, like the Conyers, come into the annals of plantation owners through marriage. William Tysen of Cheshunt, Herts., who died in 1778, owned the Bridge Plantation in Antigua, and in 1791 his only daughter Sarah married Sir John Tyrell at Hanover Square, their family spreading over Essex. The fact that detailed information of Bridge Plantation is contained in the Tyrell archives denotes some interest in the subject. An early list of slaves and their values gives Robin, driver and boiler, £72 10s. 0d., Philip £70, Frank £72 10s. 0d., Succo burst-bellied not valuable; among the women are Maria £45, Mary, one hand £30, Dian, decrepit, no value, Hanah, decrepit £6, Katterina £50, Joan old and erratic £10, Bessee, decrepit £30, the negro boys and girls, Toney £70, Jacob £65, Cippio £45, Sampson £30, Secunda £35, Nannie £45, Judeth £30, Dodie £30, Bessie £9, Frank £12. There is an item later of 'Toney, one hand', and this disability, also that of the slave Mary, were probably results of the frequent accidents in the sugar mill, though the severance of a hand was a slave punishment for certain offences. Such barbarism is illustrated in a record among the Tyrell archives of an incident on the Bridge plantation in 1756. A female slave Molly, the offspring of Judea a negro belonging to the estate, was leased out to a Doctor Bucksthorne. The letter home reporting the inhuman incident states that 'upon Moll frequently absenting herself from the Doctor's service, he cut off one of her legs, as I am informed'. The reaction to this was that Colonel Thomas Williams, attorney for William Tysen, obliged the doctor to pay the appraised value for her. 'Molly has now four children' and the question is whether Doctor Bucksthorne is entitled to the children now he has paid for the maimed mother.

From another collection of Essex records comes an account of a slave sale in which occurs a name that could be connected with the county, Nightingale. Roger Punnet, of St. Philips, Barbados, sold Edward Nightingale a negro woman Phebe, her young child Cherry, and a breeding sow, for 3,885 pounds of 'good muscovado sugar'.

But the thought of the enormous negro enslavement of

the 18th century seems so repelling to the modern mind that
one wonders what kind of people they were who supported
this giant slavery. Certainly the times were to a large extent
profligate and coarse, and with some aspects exhibited a
morality and callousness in which the finer feelings of humanity would have little place, especially when the sufferers were
in a distant country, and great wealth was involved. There
would, of course, be many exceptions to this corrupt living
with its inhibiting effect on the finer human apprehensions,
but through an Essex connection came an instance of sugar
and grossness. As a panman at Plaistow Wharf I worked with
George Beckford, an interesting young man, who claimed
descent from the greatest of the sugar plantation owners of
that century, Alderman William Beckford (1709-1770), Lord
Mayor of London, whose most imposing statue is in the Guildhall, a man of enormous wealth. The guests ate off the
alderman's gold plate, the titled personages present included
six dukes when Beckford gave a dinner at the Guildhall.
George Beckford's progenitors held the tradition that some
of the vast Beckford fortune was still existing to be claimed,
and George employed a professional genealogist to trace the
ancestral line between himself and the alderman. Among the
records examined was William Beckford's will, a copy shown
to me, the bequests including sums of money to the various
mothers of his white illegitimate children. When a younger
man on the family estates in Jamaica he had other children
by negro mothers. The great number of mulattos in the
sugar islands shows how common were the unmarried unions
of white overseers and managers with the slave women,
though not all owners had these illicit amours, and all this
is recounted to indicate a kind of moral climate in which a
tender conscience for the degraded position of the black
slave was a rare plant, especially when great family fortunes
depended on this lowly labour. In the Beckford will the
child succeeding those above was the only one born in
wedlock, William, who inherited all, and was the author of
that strange and notable book *Vathek* and the builder of
the magnificent 'folly', Fonthill Abbey; Byron pronounced
him 'England's wealthiest Son'. The father owned 22,000

acres of plantation, and after the abolition of slavery the son received £15,600 compensation for 770 slaves. George's hopeful attention to genealogical possibilities was a somewhat hazardous proceeding with such a large progeny succeeding the alderman, and the pursuit of this illusive gold could bring the seeker to the wrong side of the blanket. George Beckford's connection with sugar has had several strands, for besides employment in a refinery as a key worker, and descent from a great plantation possessor, he left the refinery for Norfolk farming, among his crops a large tonnage of sugar beet, some of which went to Tate and Lyle.

An insight into slave conditions is given by 'William Beckford, Junior', as he described himself, a second cousin of William the son of the alderman. He put in writing some observations made by him in Jamaica during his 13 years' sojourn there.[13] His suggestions for more humane consideration for the lot of the slave reveal the existing barbaric conditions. He advocated better arrangements on board the slavers, such as lessening the number carried, writing: 'Suppose a cargo should consist, as many do, of 600 slaves, and one half of them should perish from neglect, or from want of common necessaries of life, and the remainder be reduced by inanition to skin and bones, the loss is great, while a cargo of half that number will result in a small loss'. No wonder, he remarks, that the slaves have mutinied with bloody results. 'That on these voyages many have perished from want, or have been thrown overboard, or left to starve on inaccessible islands, is too generally credited to remain in doubt'.

He goes on to confirm what the reader must already apprehend, that after purchase, seasoning, and allocation to tasks according to age, sex, and condition, the lot of the slaves depends on the consideration or harshness of the owner or his deputy. The usual working hours, as detailed by him, were no worse than those of most English labourers of that time, 6 a.m. to 9.30 a.m., 10.0 or 10.15 a.m. to 1.0 p.m., 2.30 p.m. to 7.0 p.m., with Sunday a day off. But 'the white people of Jamaica believe that negroes will not work unless roused by the sound of the whip, and a half-drunken overseer will lash out all around instead of the one defaulter'. He is of opinion that no slave should receive more than the legal sufferance of nine and thirty lashes, unless it be in the presence of a doctor who should be made responsible for excesses of infliction. There are sombre records of 'excesses'.

The dawning concern over the lot of the slave shown by the last writer is exhibited by a family, of some Essex connection, owning sugar plantations in the Caribbean. Edward Jessup of Writtle Park was an 18th-century[14] owner of a big estate in St. Kitts, where he had at one time been senior Councillor, a somewhat turbulent politician. The Pinney family of Nevis, to whom reference is made below because of their Essex connection, were on friendly terms with him, for when in 1761 he made a journey to the West Indies to visit his sugar plantations he arranged for the benefit of an apprehensive John Pinney in England to visit the Pinney plantation in Nevis and give an impartial opinion on the state of affairs there. He on his return reported much that was unsatisfactory. Here is indicated a fraternity of absentee owners who did service for one another on inspection visits.

The Pinney family have interest as examples of humane slave owners. John Pinney writes of his sugar boiling hands in a manner little suggestive of servility. A boiler house, he states, should be laid out so that the overseer can see all working on the pans, but the head boiler, generally a negro, is the artist, and the quality of the sugar depended on him (a fact still true in my day of the panman or sugar boiler). 'In the making of sugar the most experienced and judicious planter had better superintend and inspect his boilers rather than dictate to them. By the practice of years, continued strike after strike, and the observation that such continuous practice cannot fail to give, the negroes must be more perfect in their business than any white man can pretend to be.' John Pinney was reduced to scolding or rewarding his boilers — he would send special presents to them when the sugars turned out well, a Christmas present of pork or beef or new check shirts. He used to lament the loss of his boiler Wilson, 'The sugar since had never been so good', and in his later years looked back on the 'golden age' when Polydore was head boiler. Nevertheless he had his problems with the negroes, and though he voiced his opposition to cruel managers he did not omit flogging on a restrained scale. His view of his labour force was 'Your own good sense will tell you they are the sinews of a plantation and must claim your particular care and attention', which shows policy intermingled with humanity, and he had no doubt of the lawfulness of slavery. When as a young man he first witnessed a slave mart he was shocked by the sight of human beings being exposed for sale. But he would argue that if God objected to slavery, he would make some sign to man. (What did Pinney expect, a black cross in the sky? He did not realise that he had been given a sign, and had ignored it, that first feeling of shock.)

A member of this family with an Essex residence showed marked considerate ownership. In the early years of the 19th century two of the Pinney estates were held by ladies of the family, both widows, and who for some time resided at Walthamstow; Mrs. Ames had the Stoney Grove estate, Mrs. Baillie the one named Symonds, and both owners wished to sell. Symonds went for a good price, but though large sums were offered for Stoney Grove sale negotiations were continually halted by the vendor till Maynard the bidder ceased attempts to secure the property. He had the reputation of cruelty to his workers and of nearly starving them, and Mrs. Ames, a pious lady, was reluctant to pass on her helpless slaves to such an owner, and though it was six years before another offer was made for the estate, though sold at a less price than that of Maynard's, though censured by her brother for such financial loss, she made it known that in retrospect her conduct in this sale was 'most satisfactory to my mind'. Consideration to the point of sacrifice by one who still believed in the lawfulness of slavery presaged an awakening humanity that was to lead to the emancipation of the slave.

CHAPTER VI

ESSEX AND SLAVE EMANCIPATION

FROM THE GENERAL INDIFFERENCE to, or even uncon-
sciousness of, the evil of slavery, there were some few but
notable exceptions from all Christian denominations and
from individual thinkers. John Locke (1632-1704) the famous
philosopher, an Essex worthy and a Unitarian, condemned
slavery by his principles of freedom. He was a thinker of
eminence who influenced many after him, and spent the last
13 years of his life at Otes, the seat of Sir Francis Masham,
and was buried at nearby All Saints, High Laver.[1] The
opening sentence of his *Two Treatises of Civil Government*,
1690, reads 'Slavery is so vile and miserable an estate of man,
and so directly opposite to the generous temper and courage
of our nation, that it is hardly to be conceived that an
"Englishman", much less a "gentleman", should plead for it.'

Daniel Defore (1659-1731) who, in spite of certain incon-
sistencies in them, held views condemnatory of slavery, had
definite links with Essex. Around 1694 he developed a brick
and tile factory in the neighbourhood of Tilbury, which for
a few years was successful, some of the brick used in building
Greenwich Hospital, and in his writings he remembers this
phase in a mixed career as happy and prosperous. A residence
near the river bank, with fine views across the water,
boating expeditions, all added to the pleasures of this period
brought to an end by the troubles resulting from some of his
political writings. Another Essex interest is that the chief
character in his famous novel *Moll Flanders* is made to spend
her years from early childhood to marriage in Colchester.

Defoe's attitude to negro slavery is that of agreeing with it
but deploring its necessity. No slaves, no sugar in quantity
enough for the prosperity of the West Indies — he agreed
with this, and for a time possessed shares in the Royal

African Company, nevertheless he came to write against abuses in slavery, as

> They barter baubles for the souls of men;
> The wretches they to Christian climes bring o'er
> To serve worse heathens than they did before.

In *Robinson Crusoe* the hero, before his island period, is first presented as a 'Guiney' trader, and in other works allusions are made to Africa, but Defoe never visited that continent; his descriptions of it were gained from friends with first-hand knowledge, among whom were the Plaistow ship's surgeon, John Atkins, and his old patron, Sir Dalby Thomas, who in 1703 became Governor-general of the African Company in Guinea. Defoe blamed long custom and undeveloped economic order for the natives selling each other.

Other notable men of the 18th century who had some acquaintance with Essex condemned slavery. John Wesley, whose itinerary preaching often carried him into the county raised his voice against the evil. Dr. Johnson, associated with Essex by a week's visit to Warley Camp on 1788, where he slept in a tent, and by a journey from London to Harwich with Boswell, spending a night in Colchester, once proposed a toast in company to 'the next insurrection of the negroes' in the West Indies, and considered Jamaica 'a place of great wealth and a den of tyrants'.

In the second half of the 18th century the feeling against slavery became organised, and in 1787 the Society for Abolition of the Slave Trade was founded by Granville Sharp (of whom more later). It met with strong opposition.

Because of the association of this religious denomination with two famous sugar families, and with myself, the strange case of the Unitarians and their attitude to slavery is worth considering. There were owners and abolitionists among them. This religious body known as Unitarianism originated in a disbelief in the Trinity, the three Gods in one, affirming that no support for this doctrine can be found in the Bible, only that God is one, regarding Christ as the greatest of religious teachers, but human. They have no stated creed or obligatory articles of belief for ministry or laity and within a wide general acceptance of some Christian and ethical principles there is room for individual freedom of belief. Some existing churches were founded 1622. Their monotheism and modern approach to religious and ethical positions divert them from the main stream of orthodox Christian belief, nevertheless this small sect, conspicuous for its contributions to social progress in England[2] had and has some notable men and women among its numbers. The fact that Sir Henry Tate, most well-known of sugar refiners, was the son of a Unitarian minister and an active member of that body gives Unitarianism a fair place in Essex sugar history, and while on the subject of noted Essex Unitarians, the name of Samuel Courtauld (1793-1881), founder of the firm of that name, can be cited, also Sir John Brunner (son of the Rev. J. Brunner) whose factory at Silvertown near the Lyle refinery, while preparing the explosive T.N.T. in 1917, blew up with enormous damage far around. My own entrance into that religious body was through attending tutorial classes and lectures on sociology and human biology by a Dr. J.L. Tayler[3] , for I gained such a great appreciation of his intellectual power that when I discovered later he was a Unitarian minister I followed him into that denomination. In my time as a panman at Plaistow Wharf I was a lay preacher from 1923 to 1966 for the Unitarian London Lay Preachers' Union, seven years its president, and in 1946-1949 was lay minister of the Unitarian church at Forest Gate. By a coincidence at that time the offices of Plaistow Wharf and Thames Refinery each held a secretary of these churches of Forest Gate and Ilford. Memories come to my mind of taking services at these and other Essex centres, Stratford, Leyton-stone, East Ham, Ilford, Southend-on-Sea, and particularly of Halstead, a meeting founded by the Courtauld family. Prominent in most reform movements of the 18th century, what was the Unitarian attitude to negro slavery? Many followed the example of the Society of Friends (Quakers) the first opponents of slavery. Among them were William Roscoe, Priestley the discoverer of oxygen, who preached a sermon, later published, against slavery, Josiah Wedgwood the famous potter, at whose works was modelled the seal of the

Anti-Slavery Society, William Smith, M.P., chairman of the Society and the grandfather of Florence Nightingale, another Unitarian (of this denomination was Sarah Flower Adams, of Harlow, Essex, author of the Hymn 'Nearer my God to Thee').

As a child I lived in the working-class area of Canning Town, some streets of which were named after the great abolitionists, Wilberforce, Clarkson, Roscoe, Rathbone. The last was a market street, and when supplanted by a modern shopping and market space the name survived as Rathbone Market. He survives in another different way — Eric Williams, president of Trinidad and Tobago, has written somewhat denigratingly of the abolitionists, as witness the first, coincidental, entry of his book:

Abolitionists (hypocrisy of),

but Rathbone emerges as the truly disinterested champion of the slave. As already stated, Rathbone was a Unitarian, as was Roscoe.

One prominent member of that denomination, Robert Hibbert (1770-1840), possessed sugar plantations employing 400 slaves. He founded the Hibbert Trust, out of which came the Hibbert Lectures, justly noted for the unsectarian approach to religion, and the scholarly *Hibbert Journal* which ran from 1902 to 1968. His father and grandfather were also associated with Jamaica, an uncle living there as merchant receiving cargoes from the Liverpool slavers, and early Hibberts supplied goods to the Royal African Company. Robert did service with a relative in a mercantile house at Kingston, Jamaica, and purchased a large estate there, yielding a large income when he returned to England. His biographer, Sir Jerum Murch[4], writes of him, 'though he was always an eminently kind master, he had no repugnance to this kind of property on moral grounds. The immemorial existence of slaves, their seeming indispensability, the influence of his early years, the long association of his family with tropical commerce, the unawakened national conscience concerning slavery' all combined, Murch considered, to explain the mind and conduct of Robert Hibbert about this institution. Through the influence of the Revd. W. Frend, opposed to slavery but considerate of the position of the young proprietor, Hibbert sent

out a missionary in 1817 in the attempt to mitigate the lot
of his slaves. He already had their regard as a generous master,
despite their complete subordination, and perhaps here was
really an example of what was often urged in support of
slavery, that they were better off than the labourers on an
English farm, but it was a condition rare enough to cause
discontent on other worse-treated plantations. The Unitarian
missionary, Revd. T. Cooper, soon realised that he was engaged
in what was tantamount to 'putting a match to a mine that
would blow up all the planters', including Hibbert, and loyalty
to his sponsor brought him home after three years. He could
perceive that education and religion would make the slaves
aware of their degraded condition, with the danger of a rebellion where they outnumbered the owners hundreds to one.
The plantocracy were also fearful of this, hence their unrelent-
ing enmity to and oppression of schools and missions in the
West Indies for the slaves.

But emancipation came, and the Hibberts received £31,120
for 1,618 slaves.[5] Robert had sold his holdings in 1836 at a
considerable loss. A relative of his, George Hibbert, many
years agent of Jamaica in England, took the lead in the construction of the West India Docks, and was elected first Chairman of the board of directors — his portrait by Lawrence
hangs in the board room of the Port of London Authority.

An aspect of owning in which the stigma of slave was not
so evident existed in this country, and had promise for the
future. In the 18th century 'English gentlemen of fashion
would include at least one black servant in their retinue', and
pictures of the period would often show the little black boy
in attendance on the lady. Most would be purchased slaves.
Sometimes a better relationship existed than that of mere
master and servant, as with the black serving man of James
Oglethorpe who could speak Arabic and was a literary curiosity among his master's friends. An Essex example of esteem
can be read upon the tombstone[6] on the east side of the
porch at Little Parndon church, inscribed to Hester Woodley,
a slave negress, which informs us she died in 1767, aged 62.
The stone was erected by John Woodley Esq.,

> As a grateful Remembrance of her faithfull dis-
> charging her Duty with the utmost Attention and
> Integrity in the service of his late mother MRS.
> BRIDGET WOODLEY to whom she belonged
> during her Life and after her Death to her
> Daughter MRS. MARY PARSONS by virtue of a
> Reciprocal Agreement made between the said
> MRS. BRIDGET WOODLEY and her son JOHN
> WOODLEY whose property she would otherwise
> have become on her Decease.

Legal ownership of the dead seems to have been made clear on
the stone! The burials of two other slaves are recorded at
Little Parndon in 1777 and 1778.[7] Some masters desired
Christian baptism for their coloured retainers[8] 'Vange,
February 4, 1711, Baptized John Tulopp, a black; West
Thurrock, Jan 29, 1721, Joseph, a black servant to Nathaniel
Grantham, Gent, aged 14 years; Grays, Sept. 17, 1734, John,
a Guinea Black, aged 25 years was baptised.

Pitsea. 1745. Francis Spenders, a Negro servt. to Captain
   Towers was baptized at Pitsey. Mr. Francis Sawel and his
   brother Cole standing Godfathers and Mrs. Sawel God-
   mother on Fryday ye ninth of August by ye Revd. John
   Pawley, Clerke.

Fobbing. July 22. 1753. John, a blackmoor servant to Mr.
   Phillips, brewer, of Ratcliffe Cross, London, who assumed
   the surname of Stanford.

This taking of the name of the neighbouring parish seems to
indicate illegitimacy. How different this 'blackmoor' entry
to the ceremonious reporting of the Francis Spenders baptism.

As recorded above Nathaniel Grantham of West Thurrock
was interested enough in his black servant to have him
baptised. Nathaniel, who died in 1723, was described as a
naval commander. Some connection with West Indian affairs
besides keeping a negro attendant seems to be suggested in
the manner of Grantham's treatment after death. Some time
ago the vicar, the Revd. J. Hayes, was inspecting a vault and
its coffins; finding one lead coffin too heavy to move, he cut
and rolled back the cover, to find within Nathaniel immersed

in a liquid and looking as life-like as if he had fallen asleep the previous night. The preserving liquid filling the coffin to the brim was identified by some venturesome person tasting it as rum, then a West Indian product.

Records of baptisms and burials of black servants appear in the church registers of other parishes. At Leyton between 1667 and 1735 were six baptisms, those undergoing the ceremony described as 'a black', 'black maid servants', 'blackamore', and one 'an East India black'. There were three burials; in 1740, Thomas, the son of Philip Bristow, a Black of Barking; in 1729, Thomas London, a black; in 1731, George Pompey, a Black Servant to Sir Fisher Tench. At Woodford about 1768 were three baptisms of 'a black', 'Black servants', and burials in 1707 of 'Benjamin Pegler, negro to Captain Brown', and in 1768 of 'Mingo, a blackamore belonging to Wido Johnson'. These last two were 'buried in woollen', a legal enforcement of the times that all burial cloths must be of wool, designed to help the wool trade. In 1635 'a negro' was baptised at Barking, and at Romford in 1688 was buried 'Cumber, a female blackamore servant from Gwyddy', and in 1741 'Arch Angel, a Black More'. Blackamore or Black More was applied indiscriminately to negro or any dark skinned person. At Woodford in 1711 a name known to us curiously crops up in a notice concerning Thomas Smith 'a well set black man' who had absconded with some money belonging to his master, Thomas Beckford.

Related by marriage to the Branfills of Upminster was William Braund,[9] and with him is connected a piece of hearsay concerning a negro servant. An underwriter in 18th-century London, when out of town he resided with his widowed sister Mary Branfill at Upminster Hall. He is said to have quarrelled with her on the subject of a black servant, left the house and later, on land purchased from her, built for himself Hactons (which still retains its Georgian appearance though let off into flats). The sex of the servant and cause of dispute has not come down with this traditional story; did such a quarrel actually occur, its cause would be interesting to students of slave history. Braund had some knowledge of the West Indies, beyond that gained by linking with the Branfills, for as underwriter he was connected with the insurance of ships voyaging to Jamaica and other parts of the West Indies. Marine insurance also brought him into contact with Samuel Bonham (son of the builder of Orsett Hall) who acted for East Indian and West Indian owners.

Not always were relations between black servant and owner good-natured, as will be seen in what could be described as the first act in the drama of slave liberation, in 1765, the scene Mincing Lane, later so much associated with the Silvertown sugar refiners. Granville Sharp (1738-1813), grandson of the Archbishop of York, has Essex interest because he was bequeathed the manor of Fairstead, the revenues of which aided the repatriation of liberated negro slaves in England. Sharp's surgeon brother William had established a surgery in Mincing Lane for the poor. On a visit here, Sharp encountered in the Lane a negro bearing the signs of a severe battering trying to reach the surgery. He was a slave brought from Barbados by his owner, David Lisle, and as a result of his master's brutal ill-treatment, Jonathon Strong, the servant, had been turned out as useless for further employment. Sharp, with his brother, restored the man to good health, fitness for work, and a situation. Lisle, discovering his former slave now well again, kidnapped him for sale to the West Indies, and in answer to Sharp's protests actually brought a suit against Sharp for stealing, an action that aroused so much public indignation that Lisle withdrew the suit. Sharp became interested in the laws relating to slaves, and in 1772, arising from the case of a fugitive slave named Somerset, secured an historic ruling when Lord Chief Justice Mansfield pronounced 'as soon as any slave sets foot in England he is free'. Some thousands of negroes had been brought home from the Caribbean with their masters for service in England, and the granting of independence caused many dismissals now they could not be regarded as property, a first indication that this canker of slavery in the body politic was not to be removed without operational pains. Sharp laboured on the problem of the discharged, for many became destitute, reduced to begging or worse, and efforts were made to return them to Africa or Jamiaca.

The work of Sharp, made prominent by court cases, increasingly drew the nation's attention to the plight of the slave, and with the backing of aroused public sympathy the Quakers began an anti-slavery movement, attracting not only Sharp but other valuable supporters, prominent among whom was Thomas Clarkson (1760-1846) who when preparing a prize-winning essay on slavery found his data so appalling that he devoted his life to abolition. He risked personal injury when visiting for information the slave-trading ports of Bristol and Liverpool. Support in Parliament was needed, and here served the cause William Wilberforce, who had been influenced by John Newton, now an active abolitionist who could supply first-hand knowledge. The long arduous campaign of these devoted men against opposition of interested parties home and abroad, the set-back to ideas of freedom by the excesses of the French Revolution, the blocking of measures by the House of Lords, finally achieved abolition in an Act declaring as illegal the slave trade, in 1808. The Navy that once guarded this industry was now employed to stop and seize the ships of those evading the new law. Slaving was now classed with piracy.

The fight was continued for the next step, the emancipation of the existing slaves, and as the years of struggle continued it became evident that the age and ill-health of Wilberforce called for another leader, and he chose an Essex man, Thomas Fowell Buxton, who continued the fight in Parliament. He was born at Castle Hedingham in 1786, and though he was an Anglican his mother was a Quaker and his wife a sister of Elizabeth Fry. We can surmise these women had formative influences on his character which raised him to grander levels of influence than that as a partner in the Truman and Hanbury Brewery. In addition to other philanthropic efforts, for 10 years he laboured on in Wilberforce's cause till at length in July 1833, a Bill to free all slaves was introduced into the Commons, and Buxton was able to assure Wilberforce, now very ill but still regardful of the movement, that the Bill would be passed. This was done in the following month, 29 August, and 311,000 slaves received freedom, their owners compensated to the sum of £20 million. Wilberforce did not live to savour his triumph, dying shortly before the event. Close to his tomb in Westminster Abbey is a memorial to Buxton.

Wilberforce's champion received a baronetcy in 1840, and died five years later, but again in 1850 a Buxton voice is raised against slavery, existing in other countries. The dislocation in the West Indian sugar industry following slave emancipation made impossible successful competition with the sugars imported by Britain from Brazil and Cuba, where slavery continued unchecked, and the double evil of the continued existence of slave-grown sugar in these countries, and its action in further demoralising the West Indian industry made the second baronet in Parliament[10] plead for restrictions on the slave-cheapened sugar. He was backed by a Colonel Thompson, who urged that Free Trade principles were not intended to encourage trade harmful to morals. They were unsuccessful, however.

Another Essex anti-slavery advocate, Benjamin Forster (1764-1829) missed witnessing the triumphal issue of many years of proselytism; man of scientific and philanthropic interests, living at Walthamstow, he was an early member of the Anti-Slave Committee of 1788.

Plaistow enters into the story of these men,[11] in connection with two places of religious worship almost opposite one another in North Street. On the south side of the Broadway stood till 1882 the largest residence in the village, Broadway House, which Robert Marten bought in 1806 and resided there till his death in 1839. He was largely responsible for building an Independent (Congregational) chapel in North Street (1807). William Wilberforce was an occasional visitor to Broadway House, also attending service in the little chapel, and a grandson of Robert Marten tells us how in one hot summer he assisted in watering the lawn, in which his grandfather took much pride, in readiness for a week-end visit from the great man, and the young hosepipe operator records proudly that he saw the celebrity.

A meeting house for the Friends (Quakers) was erected in North Street, in 1819, and in this pleasant building with its long pillared portico was heard the voice of that great prison reformer Elizabeth Fry; and that same grandson who watered the lawn, now Dr. W. Cooke, recalled the dignity of her presence and the 'wondrous music' of her voice. 'John Bright have often seen there'. (This famous statesman will enter the Jamaica saga later.) But noteworthy is that Buxton was acquainted with the meeting house. On holiday in Rome in 1839 he wrote home on Christmas Day, 'Today I have been for the first time to St. Peter's and seen high mass performed by the Pope himself. For ornament, for the display of wealth, for music, for, in short, a scene, fifty to one on St. Peter's Cathedral against the Friends Meeting at Plaistow; for religion, for worship in spirit and in truth, fifty to one on Plaistow Meeting against St. Peter's in all its glories'.

The views of Nelson on slavery have been stated; what of the great land hero, the Duke of Wellington? His reaction to abolition is obtained through an Essex family.[12] Bifrons was a pleasant 18th-century house a little south of Barking town, overlooking the levels and Gallions Reach, with parkland and gardens, the Roding flowing through its grounds, and here lived Bamber Gascoyne, M.P., owning estates also in Ilford and South Hornchurch. His daughter Frances, born in London, became Marchioness of Salisbury and acquainted with the leading political and social figures of the time, one close friendship being with the Duke of Wellington. Conversing on the *Life of Wilberforce* just published (1838) she asked the Duke if he thought Wilberforce 'had done good to the morals of society'. 'Not the least in the world' was his reply, adding that he believed Wilberforce had increased the general traffic in slaves by procuring its abolition in England. (While it is true that abolition drove the trade of slaving underground, to smuggling and other evasions, it is difficult to understand how the freeing of 311,000 slaves could add to their number.) The lady's own views on slavery are not stated, but her uncle, General Isaac Gascoyne, M.P. for Liverpool, who attended her father's interment in the family vault at Barking, was a champion of West Indian interests and connected with the Triangular Trade.

Lecky the historian considered this emancipation of slaves one of the greatest humanitarian movements known in history, and it is true that the great champions of the cause and the mass of supporters were actuated by altruistic feelings. But some influential support came from less disinterested sources, for many manufacturers, including sugar refiners, chafed at the several monopolies enjoyed by the West Indian planters and traders, and wished to see the end of these exclusive rights of trading, which would open the way for English merchants to wider areas of trade.

So deep-seated was negro slavery in the West Indian economy that it could not be excised without leaving prolonged traumatic conditions, and following the freeing of slaves came a collapse of the prosperity of the sugar islands; and the mean years that followed for the negro population, their lack of representation in administration of the island though out-numbering the whites 50 to one, led to the tragic affair known as the Morant Bay Rebellion, in 1865. It possesses such a curious Essex echo that it is now described. An examination of the Chapman and Andre map of Essex for 1777 shows shaded areas named 'Cherry Garden' at Orsett, Burnham-on-Crouch, Southminster, and South Hornchurch. The last named, near where I live, is associated with a Cherry Tree Inn, dating back nearly two centuries, a Cherry Tree Lane also old, and Cherry Tree Field occurs twice on the 1839 Tithes Map. Of course, the cherry enters into numberless place-names over the country, but this special indicating and naming of 'Cherry Garden' four times seemed to give the nomenclature a particular Essex significance despite the fact that it crops up outside the county. Consequently, when a map showed an area in Kingston, Jamaica, named 'Cherry Garden' it was natural to wonder whether the name was bestowed by an Essex settler. An enquiry on the point to Clinton Black, the Jamaican Government Archivist at Spanish Town, brought back a friendly letter to the effect that the name's originator was unknown. Around 1800 the owner was Joseph Gordon, sugar estates attorney, who had several children by his negro slave woman, and a son of this irregular union was George Gordon, who became a capable business man. Baptist preacher, J.P., and later, a champion of the depressed former slaves. His father later married a white woman and raised a legitimate family, but his business affairs declined while those of his coloured son prospered. Cherry Garden, which, among other estates of his father's, had been seized for debts, George saved by paying off the sums himself. Later, when his father decided to live in England after George had straightened out some tangled affairs, the son took over Cherry Garden.

George Gordon was to be a central figure in a tragic episode in Jamaican history that stirred England with mixed feelings for some years afterwards.[13] In 1862, Edward Eyre was appointed temporary, later permanent, Governor of the island, a hard man, an intolerant Anglican, with a contempt for the negro population, and as the clashes between negroes and administration increased, singled out George Gordon as his special enemy. When on 11 October 1865, the smouldering unrest burst into flames with ensuing bloodshed at Morant Bay, some miles from Kingston, George Gordon was at Kingston so could not be associated with instigating the riot, but on the contrary had advocated lawful rather than violent measures to secure improvement of conditions despite his vehement hostility to Governor and administration. Eyre, acting with promptitude and decision, first contained the rebellion to the St. Morant areas, then proceeded to stamp it out, but with the utmost vindictiveness. He proclaimed martial law over the turbulent area, set up courts martial, after trials at which 345 were executed, nearly another hundred summarily shot by government troops, a further 147 shot later, with innumerable floggings of men and women. Implacably Eyre pursued his enemy Gordon, and overcame the fact that Gordon was at Kingston outside the area of martial law and entitled to a proper legal trial by transferring him to St. Morant where his victim would be subject to court martial and a foregone verdict. Gordon was hanged in front of the burnt-out court house. When news reached England of what had happened, people were disturbed at the rebellion, some supporting Eyre's actions, but also many shocked at the ruthless number of executions and the illegal trying and execution of Gordon. A public demand for truth concerning the Morant Bay trouble resulted in the sending of a Royal Commission of enquiry, the findings of which gave Eyre credit for prompt action, but condemned him for prolonged excessive severity and for the miscarriage of justice in Gordon's trial and execution. He was recalled to England and dismissed from the service. The matter did not end here, for a group named the Jamaica Committee including 19 Members of Parliament with John Bright at the head, determined to bring Eyre before the courts on a charge of murder. This strange case was prolonged as long as 1872, during which time he was twice prosecuted, once for murder and once for high crimes and misdemeanours, but no jury would convict. The sides taken by famous men of the time are interesting, Charles Kingsley, Thomas Carlyle, John Ruskin, Alfred Tennyson on the side of Eyre, with Thomas Hughes (of Tom Brown's Schooldays fame), Charles Darwin, John Stuart Mill against him. Memories of the Indian Mutiny, of successful negro insurrections in other islands, were said to have actuated Eyre's fierce reactions to his own uprising, but his savagery and illegal execution of Gordon troubled Britain.

The owner of Cherry Garden did not die in vain, for his execution helped to bring Britain's attention to the condition of Jamaica, and from this time the island began to recover and commence the long journey to Dominion status. To the growing of sugar cane was added that of the banana. Then in 1937 Essex entered the Caribbean area through our Silvertown refiners Tate and Lyle, when a subsidiary of this firm, the West Indies Sugar Company, acquired estates and built sugar factories at Frome and Monymusk in Jamaica, and at Brechin Castle in Trinidad, rum also distilled at the latter island, the well known 'Caroni' product. The world-wide economic depression of the 1930s affected Jamaica and Trinidad, and Tate and Lyle did not escape the disturbances that occurred in 1937. By 1970 the two refineries of that Company, with others operating in the island, maintained the sugar industry as the chief contributor to the economic values of Jamaica. The political changes in the island may have effect on the future role of Tate and Lyle.

CHAPTER VII

THE SILVERTOWN REFINERS – I

DUNCAN, TATE, MARTINEAU

SUGAR PRODUCTION in Essex has so far been located in two places, the shadowy business at Colchester and the refining at Stratford, but processing on the grand scale, replacing the small East End businesses in supplying a large part of England's sugar, began on the Essex Thames soon after the disappearance of Stratford refining, on the former wide levels named Plaistow Marsh. The great expanse of ditch and pasture took this name from the then nearest inhabited locality, the village of Plaistow, and the nomenclature of Plaistow Wharf, mentioned in the Kohl case and the future home of the Lyle refinery, was no doubt decided by its situation on the edge of the Marsh. The lonely levels were first traversed by railway in 1847, and by the Victoria Docks in 1855. The former attracted industry to the river's reedy banks, and in 1852 settled here the factory for waterproof coats of Stephen Silver, after whom Silvertown was named. Till 1886, when it became a borough, West Ham was an Essex parish divided into three wards, the largest of which was Plaistow with its village and great marshlands, including the area of future Silvertown, so truly into parochial Essex came the refineries of Duncan, Tate, and Lyle, and despite the recent inclusion of this manufacturing neighbourhood in the greater London borough of Newham for administrative purposes, Silvertown is geographically and historically still attached to Essex.

The first of the monster refineries that appeared in Silvertown was inspired by the Greenock firm of Duncan, Bell, and Scott.[1] Around 1860 this firm, as other sugar houses, was producing a certain proportion of white sugar and large quantities of yellow, the latter in much demand among the poorer classes because of its lower price. By a development in process this Greenock company improved the usual dull yellow of moist sugar to an attractive pale primrose. It became very popular and promised to be a fortune-winner, and to exploit it to the full the firm decided to build a larger refinery on the Thames and thus arose Clyde Wharf at Silvertown. James Duncan, senior partner, came south to manage the venture, with offices at 9 Mincing Lane, and residence at Highbury. His professional talents had earned him the name of 'prince of sugar refiners', and under him the new business thrived and could produce 2,000 tons weekly. He possessed large estates on the Clyde, which would explain the naming of the London venture, and he later became the sole owner of refinery.

He was truly a remarkable man, 'in whom was blended industrial genius with religious and philanthropic zeal'. He was born 1834, son of a Glasgow bookseller, and the statement that young James began his connection with the sugar industry as a boy of 11 years old comes from a close friend of his in Silvertown days, J. Spencer Curwen, author of *Old Plaistow*, already mentioned. James showed such ability in the sugar sphere that advancement finally brought him into partnership with the Greenock firm of refiners mentioned above, and on taking charge of the Clyde Wharf enterprise he built up its business in the next 20 years till its profits reached £100,000 annually. He held a great reputation for professional sagacity in sugar refining circles, holding important posts, such as chairman of the British Sugar Refiners Committee, and his pioneer work in beet sugar production many years before its full adoption in England is related in Chapter 9. As an employer he was considerate and advanced, in those days of many working hours cutting down the working day of those engaged in hot temperatures to eight hours without a demand for this.[2] On this point of working in heat I was told by a former worker there that on the hot floors a light ale was provided for drink (known also in other refineries) and was probably an innocuous brew prepared on the premises. Duncan paid for a day at the seaside for the (3,000) employees and their families.

When he came to Clyde Wharf, the Victoria Dock region was in a seemingly hopeless state of neglect, 'band-box' houses built on former marshland, drainage into stagnant ditches, unkept roads flooded in winter and unlit, fever and ague giving a higher mortality rate than Plaistow village, neighboured by noisome or objectionable trades exiled from town.[3] This was the early Hallsville, and in Charles Dickens's magazine *Household Words* for September 1857 such a grim picture is presented of these 'Londoners over the Border' and only the poorest lived there. Duncan participated in the efforts to improve such woeful conditions, paying a doctor £300 a year to attend his men, also organising sick relief for the whole of the district, and founded or sponsored other movements for the benefit of this depressed community. The £20,000 it is reckoned he gave away (a great sum when money values of those days are considered) was mainly devoted to the Victoria Dock neighbourhood, a large portion financing church building, and in this religious activity he, a Congregationalist, displayed an astonishing breadth and tolerance of view, subscribing to all existing denominations impartially as though on the principle that any religion is better than none. To build two churches of differing denominations must be an unusual feat even among liberal Christians. Though a member of the Highbury Congregational church, he built one in 1868 for that religious body on the Victoria Dock Road, opposite Tidal Basin railway station, paid the Minister's stipend for many years, financed annual treats and excursions for the Sunday School children. Also on the Victoria Dock Road was his second church, built for the large number of his workmen who were Presbyterians. Previous to this he had provided a preacher to minister to them, then in 1873 he erected a commodious church, with school rooms, (not far from the Congregational building) at a cost of £2,000, and transferred it as a free gift to the Presbyterian church of England, together with £150 per annum for three years towards support of the ministry, continuing to give £50 a year to the minister for work among the children. The Synod of 1874 recorded their 'deep sense of the generosity displayed by Mr. James

Duncan — all the more graceful in that he is a member of another Christian Communion', and elsewhere is recorded appreciation of his 'singularly generous conduct'. As a boy I lived near the two churches, and in later years was inside both as visiting preacher and teacher.

Just before the First World War the Congregational church building showed signs of sinking, causing it to be closed and meetings transferred to the smaller halls.[4] In response to an appeal for help, the Shaftesbury Society and Ragged School Union in 1922 became the new trustees of the property under a scheme devised by the Charity Commissioners, and with this help the derelict church was transformed into the Foster Hall. The church had always been known as 'Foster's' after its first minister, Josiah Foster, who served 35 years. (The name is also perpetuated in nearby Foster Court.) In 1927 were laid the foundation stones of the Lester Institute, and at the 1928 opening ceremony the inheritor of an illustrious name was present, the Earl of Shaftesbury, president of the Society of that name. The Duncan schoolrooms survive, and are extensively used. His liberal spirit would have greatly approved of how the cause he initiated has continued into the valuable religious and welfare work of the now Victoria Dock Mission. His Presbyterian church was destroyed during the intense enemy bombing of the district in the Second World War, and was not rebuilt.

Other causes received help from this generous man. His gift of £1,000 in 1876 to the building of the Baptist Tabernacle on the Barking Road at Plaistow so 'stimulated' the effort that 'a considerable sum was raised' and work commenced; the Boyd Institute for workmen which arose in 1875 close by the new St. Luke's church at Tidal Basin has a marble tablet of commemoration with Duncan's name as treasurer of Committee, and as top donor (£500); the Roman Catholic cause received his help. A tablet with his name among others, from the old West Ham Dispensary of 1874, is on the wall of the present Queen Mary's Hospital at Stratford, which succeeded the earlier institution.

A most remarkable donation, its achieving effect because of its timing greatly exceeding its intrinsic monetary value, was that to the movement which secured West Ham Park for the public. In 1868 John Gurney, member of a family noted for its philanthropy, was owner of the fine parkland now known as West Ham Park, then named Upton Park, and wishing to sell the land, valued at £30,000 or more, but unwilling (as were many local people) to see it disappear beneath bricks and mortar, he offered the land at virtually half this price to the West Ham authorities on condition its 77 acres of parkland and gardens, noted in the past as second to Kew in arboreal excellence, be used as a public garden. The story of the effort and frustration to gain this magnificent prize is too long to be told here, till we reach the point where the last £400 is wanted to complete the purchase, but with all sources of public revenue and private subscription dried up. Gustave Pagenstecher, the zealous and responsible secretary of the movement to acquire the park was in despair, especially as he had bound himself, as 'poor as Job', to procure the money. His words seemed to imply legal penalty at this failure, 'more than once did I repent my folly in signing that fatal bond'. Then came like an inspiration the thought of Mr. Duncan, the Silvertown sugar refiner and his benefices. It seems strange he had not been approached before, but he was a quiet retiring bachelor whose gifts were made unobtrusively and locally. To Clyde Wharf journeyed Doctor Pagenstecher with his troubled tale of frustration and his own financial embarrassment, and when Duncan heard the sum outstanding he said 'Go to my cashier and he will give you a cheque for £400'. Pagenstecher wrote afterwards 'I stood in wonder and amazement and scarcely knew what to say. I shall ever feel that I owe a deep debt of gratitude to that gentleman who could act so handsomely and so nobly to an utter stranger as I was to him at that time. My mind was relieved of a great burden and the purchase of the park was now assured'. West Ham Park, so opportunely saved, was opened with great ceremony in 1874 and maintained by the City of London Corporation ever since, the West Ham authorities refusing to accept the 'burden' on the rates.

Far from his Silvertown activities were those on his Clyde district estates of Benmore, Kilmun, Bernice;[5] some near the

Holy Loch, where he planted coniferous woods over an area of 1,600 acres, and set up iron and silver mines. But it was a silver tongue that increased the Essex connection. Charles Spurgeon, the famous preacher, was a personal friend of the refiner, and with him at Benmore Spurgeon often spent holidays, while there addressing meetings of several thousand hearers in the open air. Spurgeon was born at Kelvedon, attended school at Colchester, and though of Congregational parentage became a Baptist minister and later gained the reputation of being the greatest preacher of his time, attracting huge assemblies in London.

Illustrating another Duncan interest was his very valuable collection of pictures, having an affinity with Henry Tate in this respect, which collection was destined to assist him in time of need. For neither skill nor piety could avert the misfortune advancing upon him in 1884. Germany and France, desiring to enhance their beet sugar industries, paid them such bounties that they could afford to export sugar to Britain to sell below cost price of the home product, a good thing for the people, but the ruin of many English refiners, Duncan among them. Despite the campaign against the foreign bounties through correspondence with the Foreign Office, he was bankrupted, and Clyde Wharf closed down in 1886. 'I well remember the tragic distress that this caused', wrote J.S. Curwen. A tradition existed, passed on to me by one of a family of workers at the refinery, that Duncan became bankrupt through giving away too much money – this sheds light upon the popular conception of his great generosity, but known is the real cause, above. It had been his intention as a bachelor to bequeath the Scotch estates to the public, but now they and the pictures were sold to meet financial claims upon him, the pictures realising £30,000, Clyde Wharf at a forced sale £60,000. After all debts were paid enough was left for reitrement spent abroad and in Scotland, in which land of his birth he died 1905. At Graham Point overlooking Holy Loch is a monument to him, the inscription reading:[6]

> Erected by Public Subscription to the Memory of James Duncan, a former laird of Benmore, who by his chemical research and enterprise revolutionised

the Sugar Refining Industry of Great Britain, and
by his Christian Character and Benevolence won the
gratitude and esteem of his fellow men. Born
1834. Died 1905.

J.S. Curwen wrote a heart-felt obituary for the *Mansfield
House Magazine,* which was reprinted in the *International
Sugar Journal*[7] and George Martineau refers to this 'touching
notice of my old and valued friend'.

Eight years before the Duncan failure at Clyde Wharf, a
second sugar refiner put up his factory at Silvertown, again
with the purpose to find a greater market for a new presentation of sugar. Henry Tate, son of a Unitarian minister at
Chorley, Lancashire, born in 1819, was apprenticed to grocery
and so successful was he at the business that later he owned
six shops in the Liverpool district.[8] About 1859 he switched
his interest to sugar refining, first in partnership with one
John Wright, then building his own factory at Liverpool in
1872, and six years later as Henry Tate and Sons a second
refinery was built on the Thames at Silvertown to develop
trade with a new sugar shape, the small ready-made cube, aimed
at replacing the old titler and guillotine, as the sugar loaf
and cutter were known. Henry Tate (created baronet in 1898)
acquired a rapid fortune by the quick bold adaption and use
of the new patents for cube sugar manufacture, and trust in
his judgment that the new sugar would be popular, for the
handy little blocks made unnecessary the laborious and waste-
ful cutting up of the sugar loaf. The disappearance of the old
loaf did not occur without a plaint from some grocers, that
breaking it up to convenient pieces kept their assistants occupied in the interval between customers, and now what would
they do? The refinery was built near Silvertown railway station on land formerly occupied by Campbell, Johnstone & Co.,
ship-builders, and became a leading industry in an area congested with manufactories of importance. Though of course
other familiar presentations of sugar came from this refinery,
the name Tate was always popularly connected with the cube,
and a humanised version standing squarely with sword and
shield, reminding of the successful repelling of nationalisation
in 1950, is now the trademark of the combined Tate and Lyle

Company. For another reason it is appropriate that a character of defensive fighting should be attributed to the cube, for there were times in the Tate history when owing to the destructive influx of cheap subsidised sugar from the Continent no profit was made on granulated sugar, and the cube kept the business 'head above water'. Progress has been made in cube preparation, advancing from slabs of prepared sugar cut into shapes with knives to the moulded cube with its finely-finished compact appearance; indeed, I could almost imagine a spilling of these having place in the exhibits of three-dimensional art in the Tate Gallery, to be described.

The Thames Refinery, as it was named, was a prominent building in Silvertown, and an early interest in the social life of the workpeople was the Tate Institute, built close by in 1887. But from the wealth that accrued as a result of Henry Tate's great business acumen and the labour of his workpeople who made possible the practical expression of his ideas arose one of London's famous buildings, the National Gallery of British Art, situated at Millbank overlooking the Thames, a worthy companion to the other National Gallery in Trafalgar Square. It is known as the Tate Gallery, after its donor, and indeed some encyclopaedias give it no other name. Around 1890 Henry Tate offered to the nation his collection of 60 paintings valued at the time at over £60,000, and including such well-known examples as the two by Millais, 'The Order of Release' and 'Ophelia' (the 'Boyhood of Walter Raleigh' was added later). The gift was conditional on the provision of suitable housing, which stipulation caused delay and difficulties, so that the donor anonymously gave another £80,000 for the erection of a gallery in which the paintings with other works of British artists could be exhibited. This handsome building with its Corinthian portico regarded almost with affection by frequenters of the 'Tate' was opened in 1897 by the Prince of Wales (afterwards Edward VII), and later the donor made possible eight additional galleries, his total contribution to this grand repository of British and modern works of art amounting to £150,000. So from sugar, with an Essex emphasis, proceeded what is now one of the great galleries of Europe. In 1898 Henry Tate was honoured by a baronetcy, and died the following year; a bust of him, and the Herkomer painting, are in the Gallery.

The Millbank gallery was of course his most magnificent gift to the public, but there were many benefactions other than to art, indicative of concern for education, religion, and welfare. In Liverpool, the University, college, and school benefited by his generosity, the Hahnemann Homoeopathic hospital was built and liberally endowed by him. This last example of philanthropy is characteristic of a donor of advanced ideas, again illustrated by his financial gifts to the Bedford College for Women in London at a time when higher education for women was not such an accepted commonplace as now, instanced also by his £15,000 gifts to Manchester College, Oxford, the main purpose of which college is to 'train students for the ministry in an atmosphere of reverent freedom unbiassed by doctrinal or credal bonds', at which college many Unitarian ministers received their training.

The Tate tradition of work for the public good is seen in the present time and in the Silvertown neighbourhood when one beholds the new Church Centre of St. John's at North Woolwich. With the church and vicarage is seen a modern well-equipped building for secular and social use for the local population. Of the Appeal Committee appointed to raise funds to assist in building this much needed place for religious and social activities, Mr. F.H. Tate, great-grandson of Sir Henry, was Chairman. Opened in October, 1968, the Centre has been most successful.

In 1883 a third refinery began to operate at Silvertown, Abram Lyle and Sons. This is the one with which I was personally acquainted over many years, also its story from beginning to near end is the subject of a book by a member of the Lyle family[9] and from which I have permission to quote, so an account of this refinery and its amalgamation with Tate is reserved for a later full chapter. Consideration now is given to a fourth refining name appearing in the district, David Martineau and Sons, operating at Duncan's old building at Clyde Wharf. This family has a long history in sugar refining activities, harking back to the latter years of the 18th century.[10] David and Peter Martineau, of Huguenot descent, were operating a refinery in Georgian London, established at Old Fish Street Hill in 1797. They were compelled to move out of the City area in 1807, due to the new Acts framed to lessen fire hazards. (The danger of fires at these sugar houses was a considerable one. An illustration by an artist named Schnebbelie, dated 1820, and entitled 'Ruins of a Sugar Bakery in Commercial Road, after fire', shows what was a very substantial building of eight storeys and proportionate width, now with a major part in a state of collapse.[11]) The brothers parted company, setting up separate businesses, David refining in Christian Street off the Commercial Road, and Peter in Goulston Square, Whitechapel, and while the latter refinery ended in 1873, the other under the name of David Martineau and Sons continued till the end of the century. Both sides of this sucral family evinced progressiveness, Peter in 1815 taking out one of the first patents for decolourizing sugar liquors with powdered bone charcoal, the other firm in later years sharing with Henry Tate the Langen patent for making cube sugar. David Martineau and Sons in 1891 came from Christian St., Whitechapel, to operate sugar refining in a former home of that industry,[12] Clyde Wharf, Silvertown; white granulated sugar and cubes were accompanied by the old sugar loaf manufacture. But the existence of the three refineries in the Silvertown district operated by three notable families in the sugar sphere, was not to last long, for misfortune soon struck at the newcomers, when in 1893 a disastrous fire severely damaged all of the main block of 10 floors, the roof collapsing and the walls in danger of falling in.[13] Another building of eight floors caught fire but was saved. Already that plague of British refiners, the competition of Continental bounty fed sugar had made it difficult for the Martineau firm to carry on a successful business, and the fire was the finishing touch. Though work continued, the firm in 1897 was forced into liquidation, one result being the end of commercial sugar loaf production in this country. The late Sir William Martineau, then a young man, started up a new company with the name of Martineaus Ltd. in Kingsward Street, Whitechapel, then in 1961 transferred to the refinery in Rannock Road, Hammersmith, also joining Manbre and Garton group. The Whitechapel refinery, the very road in which it stood, have disappeared beneath a housing estate and, needless to mention, the Christian Street building has gone. In my younger days some panmen from Plaistow Wharf found employment on the Kingsward Street pans.

The Martineau family were not at Silvertown long enough to add a contribution of note to the local benefactions emanating from sugar, but elsewhere David Martineau (1827-1910) who shared with George the partnership of the Christian Street refinery, was a J.P., filled public offices in South London where he resided, was a L.C.C. alderman, served on a Board of Guardians for many years, and held office as deputy Lieutenant of the Tower of London. George (1835-1918) represented the British Government on important international conferences on the sugar bounty problem and other matters, and was awarded a C.B. At the request of the publishers, Pitman, he wrote 'A little book' *Sugar* in 1910. When a young panman I remember buying this (1s.) and it was, as it deserved to be, very successful, and reached a fourth edition a year before the author died in 1919. Still with its original name *Sugar* a fifth edition was published in 1927, and this time with George Martineau's name as author appeared that of F.C. Eastick, M.A., who revised the work, particularly to include the English beet industry progress. He was director and refinery manager at Martineaus Ltd., but had a family connection with the Lyle refinery. The first chemist at Plaistow Wharf was John Eastick with no laboratory in the refinery, doing his analyses in his City laboratory till his notebook records a lab. in the 'pan loft'. His first assistant was his brother Charles who in 1890 left for Martineaus, and whose son is the reviser of *Sugar*.

George Martineau's son William (1865-1950) the founder of the resuscitated company after the Silvertown disaster, was knighted in 1935 for political and public services, continuing his philanthropic activities in the North of Scotland. His son Peter, now retired, is still a director of the Company and the grandson William became a junior executive in 1968. James Martineau (1805-1900) the noted Unitarian divine and scholar, and his sister Harriet (1802-1876) equally famous as novelist and political economist, were nephew and niece of the early David of the 1797 refinery.

With the passing of the Martineau firm from Silvertown, it appeared that sugar had finally deserted Clyde Wharf especially as it was utilised by a different industry, but sugar interest for a third time was to appear there, as described later.

ig. 2. Sugar Factory, Antigua, in the 18th century.

CHAPTER VIII

THE SILVERTOWN REFINERS – II

LYLE, BEGINNING AND END OF A GREAT REFINERY. TATE AND LYLE

FIRST JAMES DUNCAN with his primrose-coloured moist, then Henry Tate with his cubes, conferred on Silvertown something like the character of a stamping ground for sugar men with novelties to sell, further suggested by the coming of a third refining business with a speciality to market, a golden-coloured syrup which, like the other two innovations, was destined to be a fortune winner. In 1880 Abram Lyle of Greenock, sugar refiner and ship owner, drew out of other interests to build a new refinery on the Thames at Silvertown, and sent two sons, Abram and Charles, to superintend its building and starting-up.[1] The site purchased on the Thames bank comprised two wharves, Plaistow and Odams, separated by about 20 yards. Plaistow Wharf had been an oil store 'for petroleum and other hazardous goods' as an old illustration puts it, and building excavations revealed deep seeping of oil. Odams Wharf had evidently been possessed by a manufacturer of chemical manure named Odams, who followed Silver into the neighbourhood in 1852, and later built another wharf nearer the Victoria Dock entrance. The land on which the Plaistow and Odams wharves were first built was formerly owned by a wealthy butcher named Hudson who supplied George IV with meat, grazed his animals on the marshlands, and resided at Cumberland House, Plaistow (already mentioned), so sugar again touches that old building.

The area including the two wharves comprised about 11 acres with frontages to river, rail, and road, and the Lyle brothers commenced building in October 1881, starting production in January 1883, under the name of Abram Lyle and Sons. Kelly's Directory was well on the mark, the 1882 issue giving under 'Sugar Refineries' the following addresses:

James Duncan, Clyde Wharf,
Abram Lyle and Sons, North Woolwich Road,
Henry Tate and Sons, Silvertown.

The new Lyle enterprise contended with several difficulties in these early days; the Continental beet sugar which wrecked Duncan, capital melting as well as sugar, a loss of £30,000 on the first year's business; and at least once the men were asked to wait for wages because of lack of money to pay them. Of this temporarily unpaid personnel the managers, foremen, and key men were all Scots, brought down from Greenock to man the new works. However, the Lyle optimism, in spite of a bank nervous of its loan, was justified as the tide of success began to rise, and prosperity was assured.

The new refinery was considered an advanced type for the times though sugar men of today would regard its process line as somewhat primitive, and to understand this view a comparison of old and new refining methods will be helpful. The modern operations are, first, to remove the coat of molasses on the raw sugar crystals by mixing them with a low grade syrup into which mingles the molasses from around the crystals. The paste of crystals, syrup, and molasses is poured into centrifugal machines, acting like the domestic spin drier, which expel the syrup and molasses, leaving the sugar now free of the latter — this process termed 'affination'. The sugar, now lighter in colour, is then melted in hot water, and into the resulting syrup lime and carbonic acid gas added, the precipitate formed from these by chemical combination enfolding impurities from the syrup — this operation termed 'carbonatation'. The precipitate, charged with these impurities, is filtered out by passage through calico sheets, the resulting clear amber-coloured syrup decolourized by passing it through cisterns of animal charcoal. The now pure colourless solution of sugar is boiled to a paste of crystals and syrup, under a partial vacuum in enclosed metal vessels or 'pans'. Again crystals and syrup are separated in centrifugal machines, the now white but damp refined sugar finally dried in open-ended

drums known as 'granulators', which expose the sugar to a
current of warm air. The 1883 process knew not affination,
carbonation, granulation (drying), nor of course the very
extensive operation known as 'recovery', whereby the syrup-
molasses thrown off from the affination centrifugals is boiled
into a crude sugar which is mixed with raw. Procedure in that
1883 refinery was to hoist the raw sugar to the top floor of
the building, melt the sugar in hot water, filter through cotton
bags shaped like long stockings, decolourize by char,
evaporate to massecuite or paste in the vacuum pans, expel
syrup in centrifugal machines, and dry the sugar by shovelling
about a floor. The additions to the process and the ancillary
buildings came by degrees in following years.

The pan floor is usually the show-piece of a refinery for
visitors, and it was so in this early building, for one such visitor
mentioned 'four bright noble-looking copper pans'.[2] Another
writer describes them as 'turnip-shaped copper pans'.[3] The
journalistic attitude of the first writer is again illustrated by
his concentration on a detail, the sight of the baskets containing Java sugar, after being emptied at the top of the
building for melt, returning to the ground by sliding down a
slanted wire.

A useful measure of output is the weekly 'melt', the amount
of raw sugar used in that period, which rose from 800 or
900 tons in 1884-5 to over 2,000 tons in 1906, and by 1955
was over 12,000 weekly. The famous Golden Syrup also
hugely increased its sales over the years, from the few tons
per week in 1883-4, to reach 100 tons in 1889,[4] touching
1,000 tons per week in 1944, then settling to an average 800
or 900 tons. Always this syrup, known as 'Goldie', was 'over-
whelmingly important', especially when cheap subsidised
foreign sugar flooding the country made impossible profit on
granulated, and syrup alone kept the refinery going. It was a
familiar substance to me, for I spent 10 years (1915-1925)
evaporating the prepared 'liquor' to syrup thickness in a
special plant housed in a separate building.

When I commenced in 1911 my three years apprenticeship
as sugar boiler or panman on two of those 'noble' pans, three
more pans had been added, and by 1938 there were 13 of

different designs and capacities at work. Then this motley
assortment was scrapped and replaced by four monsters in a
new building; when I boiled the first sugar for market in a
fifth of newer design (1951), I could reflect that in 40 years
I had progressed from those comparatively small 'turnip pans',
each taking over three hours to boil about 30 tons of massecuite, yielding one half in dry sugar, to one that went
storming up to boil 60 tons of massecuite, yielding 40 tons
of dry sugar, in 70 minutes.

The separation of golden syrup from the pan floor into
another building in 1915 was not the only departure, for
earlier another operation, 'recovery', had been allocated in
1902 to a separate and considerable building, the Wharf
House. Its two pans increased to five as the 'melt' increased.
During my early days in that exacting Wharf House I committed my major disaster, misled by a faulty observation
glass. With the slow-boiling syrup of that department a pan
would need anything from nine to 16 hours to boil a panful
of recovery sugar, and I overloaded such a pan to an extent
that it took from start to finish over 40 hours to boil — a
record for that refinery and perhaps for any other. I was
promptly shifted from that department, with regret on both
sides, but returned some years later in charge. (My career was
not all one of calamities.)

Gradually the House became overloaded, and 'a great tangle
of pipes, valves, pumps', tanks, mixers, machinery of all
kinds; congested, hot, noisy, a strong though not noisome
smell that penetrated one's clothing, a grim place, with formerly a 'really frightful' basement. I was for three years in charge
of the pans section of this mighty maze, and from my present
retirement I look back in wonder! But all this was scrapped
in 1956 for new buildings and plant continuous with the 1938
Pan House so that the five market sugar pans and the recovery
pans were aligned in one long 'Pan Floor', immaculate,
spacious, modern-looking, indeed I experienced pride when
ushering my parties of visitors through the end door on to this
really impressive vista.

I little suspected the impending end of all this, nor did
Sir Oliver Lyle's book *The Plaistow Story* give any prescience

of it, for the book was published in 1960 and the author died in 1961, five years before the virtual end of the refinery, which regretfully I will have to record. His book is a detailed, vivid, and sometimes entertaining account of the progress of the refinery till nearly 1960, and I have drawn much upon it, by permission. Occasionally in the more serious work were commendatory comments on personnel, upper and lower grades, and my excuse for picking up the one remark of a somewhat different nature is that in it I had personal involvement. Concerning the old Syrup Shed, one of the original Odams buildings, adapted to be the department in which the golden syrup was filled into cans, he wrote, 'Most of the men who began work at Plaistow 50 years ago started [when young] in the Syrup Shed. However responsible and wise they became after graduating to melting house or refinery, they were a pack of hooligans in the Syrup Shed'. Commenting on this 'hooligan' statement under the heading 'The Syrup Shed makes good' I wrote,[5] 'Downright, but true, and I should know, for I was one of them, and I remember when first starting here looking on appalled at my future fellow-workers, and shrinking from them. Dickens at the blacking factory had nothing on this frightened boy. But those saving words 'wise and responsible' are also applicable, for just as 'out of the strong came forth sweetness' so from that unsavoury crew came not only the steady workman, the capable foreman, the skilled artisan but, ranging further, the town councillor, the preacher, the office senior, three professional footballers, the slain or decorated warrior. The social worker, confronted by the 'teen-age problem' would find hope here in discovering what can happen after the early capers'. The cause of this little homily was one of these early uncouth workers, now a respectable family man, telling me that a son of his had been inducted as curate to an Anglican church. Necessity brought me to this department in 1906 while still 14, the working day 6 a.m. to 6 p.m., with hour for breakfast and hour for dinner, on Saturdays till 2 p.m., hour for breakfast, 57 hour week for 7s. wage, carrying wooden cases from an outside chute to the workers inside. The older lads and youths were piecework with fluctuating hours and wages while a number

of adult charge-hands were on the same hours as myself at a
weekly wage of 24s. Soon after my arrival here a new foreman
Robert Tyzack, gave me a considerable lift by promoting me
to be his clerk and general assistant, which post I held for nearly four years, after which time he secured for me a position
which could lead to apprenticeship to the trade of sugarboiler
or panman, a much coveted post among the more aspiring
youths, as the one skilled trade within reach of the refinery
workers, and eight-hour shifts. I owe him much. He was a
great-uncle of that talented actress Margaret Tyzack and, sad
to relate, a victim of the Great Silvertown explosion of 1917.
This tin-filling department was later housed in a good modern
building and staffed by girls and women, so that a department
I first entered with such aversion became metamorphised
into a shining place of ingenuity with personnel pleasant on
the eye where 50 years later I could conduct visiting parties
with distinct feelings of showmanship.

In those 50 years I have noticed many changes in the
human spheres; smelly moleskin trousers and coloured necker-
chief giving way to the lounge or sports suit; the meals brought
from home in basin or plates tied in a coloured handkerchief
suspended from the hand and consumed in a dubious-
looking canteen housed in an original Plaistow Wharf shed,
giving way to good cheap meals served in a well-equipped
works restaurant; the long walk to work, often in muddy
conditions that would have made the modern shoeware
impossible, replaced by new roads, public transport, or car.
Less are the hours of work.

In this story of progress at Plaistow Wharf Refinery one
remarkable failure is reported, the Lyle venture into the
business of confectionery manufacture.[6] In 1897 a large
substantial building of three lofty floors was erected, known
as the 'Chocolate Factory', two French confectioners engaged
for control, and chocolates of high quality and other sweet-
meats produced. But despite the goodness and variety of the
confectionery, or even because of this, the business lost money
and was abandoned after two years; lack of good will hindered
competition against established confectioners, and some of
these businesses were Lyle's best customers for sugar. The

Chocolate Factory, however, later served several useful purposes, finishing with the first floor a good-class restaurant for the 2,000 strong workpeople, and the floor above a spacious recreational hall. Has now anyone other than myself eaten sweets from a tin labelled 'Lyle's Acidulated Tablets'? Robert Tyzack kept one under lock and key as a relic in the Syrup Shed.

The surrounding locality has benefited much from the generous giving of the Lyle family. In particular Queen Mary's Hospital at Stratford has received considerable financial help and personal interest. C.E. Leonard Lyle (later Baron Lyle of Westbourne) was chairman of the Committee of Management 1915-1932 and for some years deputy president and vice-patron, much of the present amplitude of the hospital attained during his chairmanship, and he also donated a motor ambulance. In 1917 his father Charles Lyle, one of the two brothers who started the refinery, gave £10,000 to the hospital, which was applied to the building of a much needed maternity block;[7] the foundation stone was laid by Charles Lyle and the finished building named after his late wife, Margaret. Another foundation stone, for a Nurses' Home, was laid by Lady Lyle, wife of Leonard, and the family interest in this important hospital has continued with her son, the present Baron, he in 1954 on behalf of the Aid Committee formally handing over the new Chapel.

Returning to Leonard, the first Baron, in earlier days he served as treasurer of the Royal Wanstead School. In addition to philanthropic work in this part of metropolitan Essex, he engaged in political activity as Conservative M.P. for the Stratford Division of West Ham 1918-1922, and the Epping Division 1923-4 (succeeded in this latter constituency by Winston Churchill). In these days he resided for some time at Coopersale Hall, near Epping Town. I remember seeing him during his routine visits to the refinery, a big man, handsome as a film star, gentle in approach. He was a tennis player of international rank, and had represented England.

As recorded, Duncan the early refiner contributed to the provision of a public park, but the Lyle family surpassed such arobreal gift by presenting to the West Ham Borough a piece of land not far from the refinery, comprising 5½ acres with 100 yards of river frontage, for use as a public recreational ground; and under the name of Lyle Park exists this pleasant Thameside garden with bandstand, lawns, flower beds, tennis courts and a terraced walk overlooking the water.

Work of public significant was that of Oliver Lyle, knighted in 1954 for services in promoting fuel efficiency; he was the author of *The Efficient Use of Steam*. His son, John is chair man of the combined Tate and Lyle Company, which combination now enters the Silvertown story. Four outstanding refiners have so far appeared, but a modern departure was a combination of two. Henry Tate and Abram Lyle, founders of the two great companies, never met though their efineries at Silvertown were barely a mile apart, and their successors continued this personal avoidance, so that the heads of the two refineries, when using the same train from Fenchurch Street for travelling to business, would endeavour to seek different compartments. Competition for sales was unceasingly keen between the two companies, though a tacit agreement, only experiencing a tremor in 1890, existed that Tate's would not make golden syrup nor Lyle's make cubes. The unceasing rivalry between the two firms, otherwise exacerbated by a third competitor, foreign sugar often subsidised, resulted in neither gaining appreciable profit from granulated sugar, golden syrup and cubes bringing in the money. A hint of change of attitude occurred during the First World War with an exchange of process experience, and after the war approaches were made for amalgamation, with its many advantages for both, and this was effected in 1921, proving very successful. Cubes and golden syrup continued in their old homes, but the granulated sugar common to both now began to show a profit, competition removed. The apprehensions of some younger members of the Lyle directorate that the old family feeling in the business would disappear in all this unifying were not realised, and all personnel were conscious of its continuing presence.

The melt of the combined Thames and Plaistow refineries increased by around 1954 to 23,000 tons weekly, a figure so prodigious that I considered it must be the record in sugar

refining tonnage for any square mile on earth. From Mr. Frank
Chapman, a widely-travelled sugar technologist, I obtained
agreement on this, the known case of two refineries or sugar
factories operating so closely as ours not producing such huge
melts, and of course no single refinery was capable of such a
colossal output, bringing back my assertion that this square
mile in Silvertown was the greatest in the world for sugar
processing.

One result of the amalgamation was the renewed linking
of the old Clyde Wharf with sugar. For some time the premises
were in the possession of the United Alkali Company, and the
lofty blocks of the former refinery buildings with the many
window openings stood gauntly between river and road. Old
Silvertown men include the unused part among their boyhood
recollections, George Beckford for instance, who with a chum
found access to it and abode in their 'Castle' (till stopped by
the police). Others somewhat older formed a rifle club there,
among the targets the many pigeons resting in the building. In
1958 Silvertown Services Lighterage Ltd., a subsidiary of Tate
and Lyle, purchased the six acres of Clyde Wharf for £145,000
as a barge-repair yard for the Company's numerous craft. The
ocean-going vessels at Plaistow Wharf were also serviced from
here. The office block on the river front with its projecting
upper windows in the centre is a pleasant blend of the modern
and the nautical.

Shipping at Plaistow Wharf was a reminder of the old Lyle
interest in this sphere. The renewal began in 1938 with the
lighterage of sugar through the formation of Silvertown
Services Ltd., and continued in 1950 with the purchase of three
steamships, which operated direct from the West Indies at a
new wharf constructed at the Plaistow Refinery. In following
years vessels too large for this refinery were berthed at Liverpool, Greenock and Canada, and steamships replaced by
modern motor-driven bulk carriers, while various companies
within the Tate and Lyle Group merged into the present
Sugar Line Ltd.,[8] operating from Clyde Wharf, and possessing
the largest sugar carrying fleet in the world. The capacities of
the vessels range from nearly 11,000 tons to over 20,000
tons, the largest built especially to operate at the new deep

water jetty at Thames Refinery which began service in 1967. The carriers bear apposite names as *Sugar Exporter*, *Importer*, *Producer*, and *Transporter*, and *Crystal Crown*, *Diamond*, *Gem* and *Sapphire*. They are mainly engaged in the carriage of sugar, primarily from the West Indies, but also from Africa and Australia, to the Group's refineries in the United Kingdom and Canada. (The 22,500 ton bulk *Sugar Refiner* was launched in 1971.)

At Plaistow Wharf even the days of sail are remembered in one small but interesting craft sometimes seen taking her load of refined sugar for the Isle of Wight. This, the sailing barge *May*[9], was built at Harwich in 1891 for the grain-carrying trade between London and Ipswich, and was acquired by the Silvertown Services Lighterage Company in 1964, who fitted her for the triple purpose of trading, apprentice training, and racing. It is economic to send her with refined sugar freights to Cowes for the Island, or with other cargoes, such as wheat, to Rochford or Faversham, while on these trading trips training is given to apprentices selected by Silvertown Services, or the Company of Watermen and Lightermen. In her ventures into sailing barge races at Southend-on-Sea, in the Medway, Blackwater and Orwell, she has won many trophies.

Among the several acts of public good credited to the dual Company was one which had particular interest for me. The Passmore Edwards Museum at Stratford, largely devoted to local natural history, was an absorbing haunt of my boyhood, and later a retreat for verification and exploration of Essex nature lore. Closed during the Second World War, the ensuing municipal economies retarded its re-opening, and to assist in opening its doors Tate and Lyle offered to pay the salary of an attendant in perpetuity and under this agreement the museum in 1953 was again made available for the public. This salary was paid till recently, when re-organisation at the Museum made the post redundant.

Suddenly to Plaistow Wharf came the end as a refinery. As I approached the age of 65, my 50th year at Plaistow (1956) and my retirement, lighter duties were assigned to me, among which was the pleasant task of conducting parties of visitors over the refinery, which I found so interesting and giving a

pleasant feeling of vicarial ownership that after retirement
with a generous pension I joined up with the little band of
pensioners who were assisting in this guide work on a volun-
tary basis. The occasional visit to the refinery for this agreeable
purpose was of service in softening the otherwise total break
of retirement, the severance from a life's work. How hugely
permanent seemed the great plant-laden departments of the
refining processes as I conducted my wondering visitors
through them, as sure of duration as, say, the Bank of England.
In 1966 came the meeting at which employees were informed
that sugar refining was to end, and in March my own notice
confirmed this. The company proposed in about two years'
time to discontinue the process of sugar refining at Plaistow
Wharf and to operate a continuous seven days a week process
at Thames Wharf, Liverpool and at Greenock. 'We are sure
that this news must come with a feeling of regret to all Old
Plaistovians, but we hasten to assure you that there are no
changes in the pension arrangements which are already in
existence'. The reasons given for this change contained some
urgency, for with sugar sales reaching across the United
Kingdom, such a heavy concentration of processing in the
South of England was now undesirable, and the new line-out
of refineries would even out distribution, also week-ends of
idle plant were to cease. The once busy Plaistow Wharf was
reduced to golden syrup manufacture and filling of sugar
packets, the materials for which were brought from Thames
Refinery.

The consideration shown in my letter for the feelings or
apprehensions of pensioners was evidenced also towards the
working personnel, the older given the chance of earlier
retirement with pension, the less old with the choice of
absorption in one of the three working refineries, or to leave
the Company with compensation. As forecast, the run-down
took two years, the last pan of sugar ceremoniously boiled on
12 April 1968. The usual pensioners' party, 300 strong, was
held on 24 April, and from it I stole for a farewell visit to
that once grand Pan Floor, now ended. By the long row of
pans, those silenced giants, I stepped in a reflective mood,
remembering how I had exercised an ancient skill upon them,

conscious of many memories, while a last tiny indicator blinked redly, like the eye of some expiring monster. It was indeed farewell. When I again left the party, a year later, the massive array of plant had gone.

So with sugar Silvertown has returned to the position of over a century ago, one sugar refinery. But how different from that early Duncan effort, with its boasted 2,000 tons weekly. The Thames Refinery with its continuous working should reach 25,000 tons weekly, the largest output, it is believed, of any refinery in the world.[10] Approaching this amount, the refinery achieved its record melt of 23,822 tons during the week ending 8 November 1969, a cause for celebration. The sugar melted was chiefly Australian cane and home grown beet sugars.

The familiar names of Tate and Lyle now indicate a group of companies producing sugar in the United Kingdom, West Indies, Africa, and Canada, with interests on the Continent, and activities, not all of sugar, in other parts of the world.

CHAPTER IX

BEET SUGAR AND ESSEX

THE BEET FOLLOWS the sugar cane in importance as a sugar producer, and its history in Britain as a sucrose yielder begins in Essex. As far back as Roman times it was known that a certain beet, Beta Maritima, had a sweet content, but not till the 18th century came awareness of its sugar yielding potential, when in 1747 a Berlin chemist, Marggraf, produced crystals of sucrose from the humble vegetable, winning for himself a niche in the history of food, changing the need of warmer conditions for those of an English field to produce sugar, his ounce of sucrose from a pound of dried white beet beginning the revolution. The discovery attracted wider scientific attention, and Frederick the Great financed further development so that the first beet sugar factory was established in Silesia in 1801. But the real impetus to this new industry came from Napoleon, his cane sugar supplies cut off by the blockade of the British Navy. Taking advice from the French chemists to try this alternative source, Napoleon encouraged cultivation and processing of the new sugar to the extent that before the end of the war in 1815, 213 factories were totalling 4,000 tons annually. When the French scientist produced the first loaves of white sugar from the beet, he was awarded the Legion d'Honneur.[1] We were to learn Napoleon's lesson a century later, when we in turn found our cane supplies menaced by sea warfare. But in the early 19th-century years, although beet sugar production became a settled industry in several Continental countries, in Britain the long establishment of cane sugar refining, the many enterprises and fortunes connected with it, supplies guaranteed by the impregnable Navy, not only made any other source of supply unnecessary but also unwelcome, and beet trials drew hostile comment in Parliament.

The scene of the first commercial attempt in Britain to produce sugar from beet was the small village of Ulting, near Chelmsford, and here in 1832 Robert Marriage, a Quaker and member of an Essex family, decided to give expression to his anti-slavery feeling by supplanting slave-grown sugar by home produced beet. He owned several parcels of land on the banks of the Chelmer and Blackwater Navigation or Canal at Ulting,[2] between Maldon and Chelmsford, and he with like-minded partners built here near Hoe Mill the first beet sugar factory in the United Kingdom, operating as Marriage, Read and Marriage, the two Marriages being Robert and James. A strange event, this, in the history of sugar in this country, that a new source should be started for an altruistic purpose, to counteract a human evil, slavery, connected with the established source. The Ulting enterprise was short-lived, under two years, financial troubles one reason for the failure, though other inimical influences were at work as will be seen. As the first pioneers in beet sugar production, this Essex family of Marriage have an important place in Essex and sugar history. Robert was a descendant of Francis Marriage, of Stebbing, who joined the Quakers in their earliest days, and died 1699, leaving an only son William, born at Partridge Green Farm[3] in 1668. William married Ruth Woodward of Mundon Hall, and through this union the Ulting property came into the Marriage family, later to Robert. The family were landowners, millers, and farmers in central Essex, Robert was all three as he possessed Hoe Mill. The Ulting overseer's rate book shows Robert J. Marriage rated on farm and Hoe Mill from September 1829 to 1832, then a sugar factory is also rated in his name. The factory appears again in the accounts the following March, then disappears. No trace of the building remains on the quiet bank of the now almost unused canal, only names as memory, as Sugar Bakers Hole for the angler,[4] and the four Sugar Mill Cottages adjoining the factory site. Even these dwellings are not the original ones that were no doubt built in conjunction with the factory and first bore that name, for the present block of cottages bears the date of building, 1870, and the initials E.C.B.P., of E.C. Brook Peachel, who bought the estate in 1857.[5] The dwellings,

I am informed, were first named Hall Cottages, no doubt in
reference to Ulting Hall, and when the sugar mill cottages
were demolished, took over the sugar name, now the official
address (though letters will sometimes bear the other
address).

This gallant adventure of ethics and sugar deserves a shrine
in the history of sugar, and not only in England, for it is
doubtful whether anything like it has occurred elsewhere. A
report concerning it states 'a desire to obtain the best information, and to promote the abolition of slavery, by producing
an article of free labour, lately induced several young men of
Essex, members of the Society of Friends, to visit France and
qualify themselves for establishing a sugar manufactory in that
country. A company was formed — Marriage, Read and
Marriage — and a building fitted up at cost of about £2,000'.
Another report states that after several visits to France, the
promoters 'engaged into their service two natives of France,
who well understood the process'.[6] The factory was 'fitted
upon the most modern principles, the metal used in pans
and other utensils being copper, the heat conveyed in every
department by steam, which not only ensures the article
from being burnt, but also removes most effectually the hazard
experienced in our sugar boiling houses, where conflagrations
have been attended by great losses to public bodies as well as
to individuals'. Follows a description of the process — the
roots are 'drawn' and rasped, crushed to a pulp in a mill, the
pulp put into bags, which are then subjected 'to a pressure of
about 100 tons', the expressed liquor boiled to the consistency
of molasses, which is then clarified 'much after the system
pursued in the London boiling houses'. The factory employed
30 persons 'including men, women, and children'. The benefits
to agriculture are enlarged upon: 'the pulp taken from the
press has much the appearance of oil-cakes' which retains a
fattening quality for cattle. 5% of sugar from the beet is
stated. Lack of capital is reported to have ended the business.

A second factory was erected on the Thames bank at
Chelsea[7] for which a large area of beet was sown at Wandsworth, and there were plans to manufacture brown paper
out of the residual pulp. This project, like that of Ulting,

had a short life, lack of capital one reason already advanced, but in addition it was 'overlooked by promoters that production of sugar in England was liable at least to the same excise as the West Indian duty-paid product'; in fact, the duties imposed were heavy. Also from the start Great Britain was definitely hostile, regarding it as a menace to established policy, the advantages to agriculture ignored. As an example of opposition is cited Dr. (later Sir John) Bowring, Unitarian and statesman, Governor of Hong Kong in 1855, author of the famous hymn

> In the Cross of Christ I glory
> Towering o'er the wrecks of time

A question of his in Parliament was 'he understood a process of the manufacture of sugar from beet had lately been brought into the country and wished to know if the Chancellor of the Exchequer was acquainted with the fact as, if successful, it might be necessary, as it had been with recent cultivation of tobacco, to pluck up the beetroots by the roots'.[8]

Enquiries placed with the Chelsea and Wandsworth librarians revealed that no record whatsoever exists of the London beet sugar enterprise, but fortunately the Ulting venture has some documentations. With Mr. and Mrs. Chartres I spent an interesting time in this parish, first seeing the old church on the canal bank, over which we were shown by the vicar's assistant curate, Sir Ivor Beauchamp, then on to Ulting Hall, an ancient capacious residence, now farmhouse, the property of Edward Arnold, but tenanted by John Payne his manager whom I had known when a manager at Wennington. A pleasant time here became profitable when a map was produced pin-pointing the site of the sugar factory by name.

Once aroused, interest in beet sugar seemed to continue and the next venture was in Queen's County, Ireland, in 1850, which seems to have been promoted by a London company, now with a commercial interest. This also was short-lived, and some reason for its failure, and that of the Quaker attempts, is contained in a paper read by Professor Hancock[9] at a meeting of the British Association in 1851, entitled 'On the prospects of the Beet Sugar Manufacture of the United Kingdom'. He mentioned the Irish company and the failed

Ulting enterprise, and then 'A manufactory had been recently established at Chelmsford, and contracts had been entered into with the farmers in that neighbourhood'. Enquiries at the Essex Record Office and examination of the county directories revealed no mention of any beet sugar factory at Chelmsford or neighbourhood in 1851 or afterwards, and it seems that the project did not get beyond the initial stages. The professor asserted that the lowered cost of cane sugar through the proposed manipulation of duties, the State-protected beet sugar from the Continent, would as competitors ensure that 'the manufacture of beet sugar could not be profitably carried on in the United Kingdom'. 1851 was the year of the Great Exhibition, and from some reports it can be seen that to the economic damning of beet sugar was joined national feeling against it. France, Austria, Prussia and Russia in that order received medals for beetroot sugars which disturbed some commentators, one writer reminding us that it was connected with Napoleon, our great enemy; that it was supported in countries of high protective duties, at a variance with true and enlightened principles of commerce; the awards were extremely unfortunate as likely to encourage enterprises of this sort. The final hope was 'that the introduction of the fabricated article as a substitute for the genuine article will be made still more unnecessary by reducing restrictions on refiners of cane'. The contrasting words 'fabricated' and 'genuine' are pretty journalese, applied to sugar.

But despite the fiscal and competitive obstacles, the prejudices against it, a beet sugar undertaking of a longer duration, beginning 1868, brings Essex back into the picture, with the ubiquitous James Duncan of Silvertown erecting a substantial factory at Lavenham in Suffolk, on the banks of the river Brett. His experimental zeal and his belief that the industry would help the rural economy led to this pioneering effort, the second in England, and with Essex largely concerned; Lavenham probably was chosen for the factory site because land there was cheap and good for beet growing, and a new railway line would provide transport.[10] The modern method of extracting juice from the beet by diffusion, i.e. soaking the shredded vegetable in hot water, had not yet been introduced in beet processing, so at Lavenham the juice was obtained as with cane, by pressure. The roots were pulped and bagged, the bags then subjected to hydraulic pressure; after carbonation and filtering; the juice was decolourized by animal charcoal and boiled to a thick syrup. This was filled into puncheons (barrels containing 2¾ cwt.) and conveyed by rail to Clyde Wharf, where it was mixed into the refining process of raw sugar. There is some reason to believe that some metal containers of carboy shape and a capacity of 300 to 400 cubic feet were also used in this transport, a number of such existing at Tate's Silvertown refinery known as the Lavenham receivers, and may have been acquired when Clyde Wharf broke up. The Lavenham factory, built on a capital expenditure of £12,000 and designed to process 20,000 tons of beet annually (an optimistic estimate never realised) began well but in its succeeding years of life met increasing difficulties that daunted even the indomitable Duncan. Failure of farmers to deliver consistently the amount of roots expected, local authority's objection to effluent in the river, local opposition extending even to sly sabotage, the serious competition of bounty-fed foreign beet sugar, caused the abandonment of the business in 1874. In 1884 Messrs. Bolton tried revival of beet sugar production here, but crop difficulties soon closed the factory again. The building was sold and used for other purposes till a destructive fire in 1905, and was finally demolished in 1960, all that remains of a great venture a few wooden piles in the river. The machinery, sold to a German firm, realised £5,000 and is said to have reached South Africa.

During 1866-9, the Metropolis Sewage and Essex Reclamation Company experimented with sewage irrigation at Lodge Farm, Rippleside, Barking, and among the crops so fertilised was sugar beet,[11] but we have to discover if and where the beet was processed. (At some time there were crops at Ilford.)

Although no large scale attempts were made after Duncan's, the idea of the United Kingdom producing its own sugar with beneficial reaction on farming was not likely to be forgotten (especially with a flourishing industry operating on the Continent) despite the Essex set-backs. But one of the most

striking features of the history of sugar is the length of time
Great Britain remained without home-grown produce.[12] The
chief reason was the artificial condition created by European
governments anxious to foster their own sugar beet industries;
combinations were allowed to set a high price on the sugar
sold to their own people, which enabled the manufacturers
with such great home profits, plus a bounty from the government, to export the surplus to England below cost price,
causing havoc among our refiners and making home-grown
beet uncompetitive. Not till the Brussels Convention of 1903
were these excessive bounties abolished. But to compete
equally with cane, beet sugar must be subsidised in any
country, and the United Kingdom was about to commence a
large scale experiment without parallel in the history of this
country, direct State subsidisation of a new industry. After
observation of certain schemes of production the Board of
Agriculture and Fisheries in 1911 made official pronounce-
ment that the production of sugar from home-grown beet was
a feasible proposition. The first modern beet sugar factory was
erected at Cantley, Norfolk, in 1912 followed by Kelham (with
Government assistance), but Napoleon's lesson was not fully
learnt by us till the First World War with the almost complete
disappearance of European supplies. By 1928, with Government aid, 18 factories were at work, mostly in eastern England,
and during the Second World War supplied all the nation's
rationed sugar, outside cane and beet supplies cut off or
precious cargo space yielded to other urgent supplies. Come
to stay had this new addition to the rural economy, a useful
fresh rotational crop, a cultivation beneficial to the land, new
cattle foods, another outlet for the farmer. Financial grants
to enable the sugar to sell at the same price as the more
economically produced cane sugar are also motivated by its
proved worth as a wartime reserve supply. In this industry
Essex has been represented since 1925 by the establishment
of the Felsted factory. But indirectly the county touched
the industry before this, when in 1923 the encouraging Government granted a subsidy to home-produced beet sugar at
26s. 10½d. per cwt., twice the value of the sugar. To share

in this 'golden gift' Tate and Lyle among other interests erected a factory at Bury St. Edmunds in company with a Hungarian group possessing expert knowledge. It became the best of the British beet factories, and among the personnel were many from Plaistow Wharf.

In 1936 the 18 factories were all joined together by Act of Parliament into a single company, the British Sugar Corporation, controlled by a Board of Directors including three Government representatives, and Tate and Lyle withdrew from beet operations, though some Plaistow Wharf men remained at Bury St. Edmunds. Thus in three ways the Silvertown refiners have engaged in the beet sugar industry. First, by processing foreign raw beet, the Lyle records showing large admixtues of this with cane, in fact from 1894 to 1903 the melt being 100% beet, at a time when the artificially fed industry was producing nearly two-thirds of the world's sugar; second, processing the harvested beet into market sugar at Bury St. Edmunds and elsewhere; and now experimental growing of sugar beet at Cosford Abbey, Norfolk, though Tate and Lyle under present regulation cannot engage in actual beet sugar production in this country. James Duncan worked a fourth approach, producing heavy syrup from the beet at Lavenham and refining it at Silvertown.

Our main Essex interest in beet sugar lies now with the Felsted factory, of the British Sugar Corporation. With Mr. and Mrs. Chartres, I spent a full and interesting day at the village, now for over three decades associated with sugar production, but famed more for its ancient school. In the morning at Princes Farm Mr. Gordon Crawford showed us the 'Forcaster' at work, the most advanced beet-harvesting machine, and far from the days of hand-digging of obstinate roots is the operation of this mechanical giant, also an advance on machine harvesters needing an accompanying lorry in which to deposit the uplifted beet. The Forcaster is an Essex development, and is constructed as a compact unit, carrying the extricated beets to a receiving space at the top of the machine, detaching earth or mud en route, at the same time slicing off the tops of the next row of beets preparatory to lifting. Only when full did the harvester go off to deposit its contents in a lorry, thus one man only was needed for the actual harvesting; in early days, several laboured at an arduous and unpopular toil. The crops, destined for the nearby factory, are grown from seed supplied by the buyers to ensure uniformity and quality. Mr. Crawford harvested his first sugar beet with a pair of horses in 1930, and he is a member of the family formerly of Suttons Farm, Hornchurch, the site of the R.A.F. Station.

Passing a 20-ton stack of beets ready for carriage to the factory at its appointed time, we made our way to the School, and were conducted over its well-appointed classrooms, workshops, its buildings old and new, the impressive chapel, our sugar interest in this well-known public school, founded 1564, lying in the knowledge that the Cromwell boys came here, that known important people in the sucral world had been educated here, that some employed at the factory had sons in the school, that neighbouring farms were growing sugar.

During the day we had observed the lofty buildings of the B.S.C. establishment with its plume of white smoke, and later its dominance in the scene when lit up at night. One writer[13] has remarked that with a favouring wind the factory smell carries for miles around, and a former woman member of the office staff recalled her strongest memory was of the 'sickly sweet smell you couldn't get away from', but though beet processing has its characteristic odour, as does a refinery, our party were not conscious of strong odours, either in or out of the buildings, though I questioned a girl on this point, knowing from experience how responsive young women are to sugar smells, pleasant or unpleasant. The warmth of the building was felt by her, not to a too troublesome extent. On commencing this conducted tour, we were made aware of the fact that this was a factory in the country when we were informed that the visiting party in which we were included would be the last for a long period, as a precaution against the foot and mouth epidemic appearing in that region.

The factory tour showed the cleansed beets pass to machines slicing them into strips, a glimpse of the revolving drums in which the strips yielded their sweetness into water (diffusion), the resulting thin syrup or 'juice' charged with lime and carbonic acid gas which combined to form a precipitate trapping impurities in the juice (Carbonatation) the extraction by filtering of this precipitate, a second carbonatation and filtering, the juice treated with sulphur dioxide to a neutral reaction, the concentration of juice containing 15% sugar to syrup containing 65% sugar under vacuum in huge boilers or vessels called evaporators, another close filtering, no char, and the rest of the process as described in a refinery, with vacuum pans, centrifugal machines, final drying. At one point I was able to chat with my former opposite numbers, the panmen. Some good interior photographs were included in an article on the factory by S.M. Jarvis,[14] the co-author of *In Search of Essex*.

This huge Essex successor to the ventures of Marriage and Duncan treats annually over 300,000 tons of beets from 23,000 acres spread over Essex and surrounding counties from Cambridge to Kent, and each day can process 2,500 tons of beet to yield 350 tons of white sugar, 250 tons of dried pulp or pulp nuts for cattle food and 130 tons of molasses for industrial and other uses. (An acre of beet will yield from 38 to 40 cwt. of sugar against the 8 to 12 tons per acre from cane; and the sugar content of the beet is 15% to 16%, the cane about 13%). The personnel of 325 men and women operate the process continuously day and night for approximately 120 days, each season or campaign from about late September to end of January; and this seasonal labour force is recruited from the surrounding locality and from Ireland. Delivery of beets to the factory is by road, though in the past some cargoes in sailing boats travelled from Walton to a suitable point for Felsted. Some other notes from the past may be related.[15] The 1953 record of 14¾ tons of roots per acre was passed in the long drawn-out campaign of 1960-61 by the yield of 15¾ tons per acre, the sugar content about 15.3%. The winter of 1962 brings out a comment on the large number of bolting (running to seed) sugar beets, very undesirable in a load. The 1962-3 campaign was noteworthy for the fact that Felsted was the last factory to finish, to give farmers opportunity to move their frost-bound crops in that freezing winter; frost when mild can be an ally to the farmer by breaking up the ground, but if long and severe can damage the beet, and in this campaign some crops remained ungathered. More cheerful were the conditions the following campaign, the beet coming of the ground clean with a good sugar content, and the factories finishing by Christmas (1963). The 1965-6 campaign was a very full one, 335,000 tons of beet processed, 55,000 tons more than the previous year, the acre average 15.5 tons compared with 12.7 tons, the sugar content 15.8% less than the previous year by 1.5%; early hard frosts, water-logged fields, made harvesting very difficult, some loads sent back as unfit for process, and there was advice from the factory that beets need as much care as potatoes when clamp-ing in wet weather.

Mrs. B. McArdle, who mentioned the 'sickly smell' has provided me with some other early memories of the Felsted factory where in her early 20s she was employed as a comptometer operator in the 1927 and 1928 campaigns. In those days no refining plant existed and she recalls the piles of brown sugar to be sent to Tate and Lyle. The small office had a canteen attached for the clerical and similar staff of 12; she can remember that wellington boots were worn for the necessary journeys to muddy and wet floors where the beet was washed; and writes of having to work out prices for the farmers according to sugar content of beets, and allocating molasses on the amount of beet sent in. She lodged at a farm near the *Flitch of Bacon* in Little Dunmow, where only one shop existed, and without public transport the journey to and from the factory was a fair walk, unless a lucky car picked her up. Apparently there was little time for amusements as she worked 'fairly late', also Saturday and Sunday mornings when the beets were coming in; but a hard tennis court was outside the office, there were whist drives and dances in surrounding villages, a cinema at Braintree where you had to book your seat and the music was supplied by one tinny piano, and the manager sprung a party at his home for the staff. She was young and evidently found her situation not uncongenial, for both in her letters to me and to the *Essex Countryside* she writes of a 'happy time of long ago' and 'pleasant memories of the happy time I spent at Felsted'. She was also surprised by modern photographs of the factory, 'how it has grown and how elegant it now is'. Praise indeed!

CHAPTER X

OTHER SUGARS AND OTHER MATTERS

SO FAR, detailed consideration has been given to the familiar sugars used by us in visible form, as honey and cane-beet sucrose, but others are compounded in our food and drink by the manufacturer, such as glucose derived from starch, present in confectionery, ice cream, mineral waters, articles of food, and medicines, while the brewer uses special sugar preparations. That a commonly-used sugar as glucose is made from starch may seem surprising, used as we are to the thought of sugars processed from plants, till it is realised that starch is also a plant-derived carbohydrate, to which chemical family all our sugars belong. The change from starch to glucose is effected by treating the substance with dilute acid, this agent afterward neutralized.

By this widening range of sugars other Essex links occur, as in the following brief biography of a remarkable personality who had residence at Wanstead, sugar interests at Stratford, and two sons at the Felsted school.[1] Albert Eustace Berry, educated at Owens College, Manchester, entered the St. Helen's laboratories of the United Alkali Company. The young man advanced to chief chemist and head engineer, possessing pronounced talent for process-improving experimentation. In 1897 he sent off an application for the position of chief chemist at the London works of A. Boakes, Roberts & Co., but when the United Alkali directors gained knowledge of this, there came the injunction of 'Don't let him go!' and a doubling of his salary. Into the hesitancy caused by such financial improvement and the gratifying recognition of worth came Mr. Roberts himself, for such was A.E. Berry's reputation that this London director travelled to St. Helens to persuade Berry that his proper place was in the metropolis. As a result of this counselling, the position was accepted in the A. Boakes, Roberts factory in Carpenters Road, Stratford, and though the works were comparatively small, employing 50 people, the directors gave the new man freedom and opportunity for research into the use of different sugars and caramel for the brewing industry. From his continual seeking of improvement and innovation in processes he took no holiday for 13 years. Not surprising that with such dedication he became works manager, from such higher position continuing to promote the interests of the company, an instance of such zeal being the acquirement, in which he was active, by Boake, Roberts of an adjoining sugar business in Carpenters Road, the Johnson Saccharine Company (saccharine was the accepted term for glucose, not to be confused with saccharin, the non-sugar sweetening substance) and the combined businesses were formed into a new company, Sugar and Malt Products Ltd., with A. Berry as manager. He could foresee a future for preparations of sugar needed by the brewers to meet a change in popular taste, for a lighter, sweeter, more palatable drink instead of the heavy bitter malted beers, the cause of much drunkenness (indeed in past days it seemed to be a practice of some innkeepers to have on sale small packets of sugar for those who wished to ame-liorate drinks). He participated in meeting this need to such an extent that after the First World War larger premises were needed. The opportunity for such an en-largement of premises and trade came through the failing state of the Manbre Saccharine Company of Hammersmith, a glucose-manufacturing firm commenced by a Franch-man, Alexandre Manbre, who, like Albert Berry, had endeavoured to replace the old bitter, strong-malted, hop-laden liquors with a lighter, sweeter drink. Proposals to absorb this weakened business had already been considered by another firm, Garton, Sons & Co., operating about two miles distant in the Hammersmith region on similar products for the brewers, and possessing the largest plant in Britain for processing glucose from maize, but no decision was reached. But Albert Berry, on investigating this Manbre business, found that by measures against preventable waste it could again pay a dividend, and such was his reputation for professional acumen that Barclays Bank were willing to trust his judgment to the extent of a £350,000 loan for which Manbre was acquired in 1919. A. Boake acted as chairman and Albert Berry as managing director of the new enterprise arising from this fusion, the Manbre Sugar and Malt Co. Ltd. The bank was repaid as the new business flourished, to which Greenock and Liverpool concerns were added.

Albert Berry had been residing at Wanstead, and probably the fact that the family home was already in Essex determined the school for his sons, Felsted, entered by Eustace in 1910, followed later by the younger son, Derbe, so again our Essex sugar saga touches upon this famous school, for the brothers educated here were later to wear the mantle of the father.

There comes another notable name through Albert Berry, when he established friendship with Richard (later Sir Richard) Garton, an association which no doubt helped on the inevitable merger into a new company, Manbre and Garton; of this Sir Richard acted as chairman, his friend Berry as managing director, till on the retirement of the former, Albert Berry assumed both offices. He had the Garton friendship on one side, on the other was a link with Lyle. When Leonard (later Lord) Lyle contested a West Ham division as Conservative candidate for Parliament, Albert Berry actively supported him and they became firm friends.

Under Albert Berry's management Manbre and Garton started bulk delivery by tank wagon of liquid sugar; powdered glucose was perfected as a highly purified form of sugar for medicinal purposes; while absorption of other companies expanded business into a further range of products, as sugar candy, coffee crystals for the Royal Household, cattle foods and maize oils, starch and cornflour from South Africa, and dextrine for glue making. A major inclusion was the purchase of 97% of the shares of the Sankey Sugar Company of Earlstown, Lancashire.

A contribution of national value was made by him in the preparation of that medically-important substance, penicillin.

During the Second World War, the need for larger quantities quickly obtainable became urgent, and to meet the problem he experimented in producing starch-derived liquors favourable to the growth of the precious mould, in this so successful that in 1942 the first efficient sample of 2 0z. was sent to the Oxford workers. From this small beginning came increase to 300 tons a year to the penicillin manufacturers, in 1945 the figure 1,500 tons, in 1950 far exceeding this.

In 1950 he relinquished the position of managing director, but continuing as chairman, keeping still in daily touch with affairs, made easy for him by the appointment of his two sons, Eustace and Derbe, as joint managing directors, who interest us, of course, as being Felsted-educated. Eustace joined the Company in 1922 and elected director in 1928, Derbe came into the Company in 1928, on the Board in 1934, and Chairman of the Board in 1968 of Manbre Sugars Ltd., controlling three refineries in London, Lancashire, and Scotland, Mr. A.E. Berry died in 1961.

Two sugar companies operating so near Essex as to overlook it across the dividing rivers justify inclusion in this 'other sugars' survey. Fowler Ltd., have been situated at Glasshouse Wharf on the Lea at Blackwall for many years. The two brothers Fowler, hailing from Glasgow, began in a small way with liquid invert sugars for London brewers till 1902, when Alexander, now alone, formed the company Fowler Ltd. The techniques of refining syrups and treacles were developed, and brewing sugars and caramels were produced with widening range of sales. The name Fowler is popularly most associated with the 1 lb. tins of 'West Indian Treacle' seen in the shops, a dark-brown product of cane sugar.

On the Woolwich bank of the Thames, opposite Thames Refinery, is Albion Wharf, where the Albion Sugar Company operate. The company was formed in 1929, purchasing the Wharf from the Admiralty, it being in the Royal Dockyard area, and produced invert sugar in liquid and solid form for brewers. In 1935 began the preparation of glucose from maize starch for confectionery and other manufacturers, and a new development was a milling process to convert imported maize into the starch required for the glucose manufacture. The name of this company and its wharf occurs elsewhere in the neighbourhood, for the main road passing the dockyard at this point was from its construction in 1842 to 1937 named Albion Road, nearby is the Albion public house first mentioned in 1848 and now rebuilt.

With a visiting party I toured one Essex receiving end of the brewing sugar described above, the old-established brewery of Ind Coope at Romford, where could be seen samples of the used candy, caramel, invert and cane sugars.[2] This last is preferred to beet for keeping the yeast active in the fermentation process, a rare example of cane selection for a special function, for now the old prejudice against beet sugar in bee food, home wine-making, and other amateur products has disappeared among practitioners of today; the chemical formulae now are exactly the same. The dominant sugar in brewing is maltose, obtained by steeping barley grain in water and encouraging it to germinate, whereby the starch in the grain is converted into maltose, the grain then dried to stop further development, and now known as malt. The maltose when aided by other sugars put in solution gives the desired alcohol in beers, fermentation breaking down the sugar into carbon dioxide and alcohol. Maltings were familiar buildings in most towns and villages, a particular Essex interest resting in the Abbey Mills at Stratford. The Cistercian abbey of Stratford Langthorne, existing from 1135 to the Dissolution, covered an area from the parish church to the Lea banks, and owned seven tidal mills, power for which explains the meandering streams flowing out of and back to the river, and the flour from here supplied much of London's bread, the Stratford bakers, men and women, displaying their wares at the appointed market place, Bread Street. In 1727, when the operating mills were reduced to three in number, a new owner introduced another use for maltose-derived alcohol, the distilling of spirituous liquors. This was near the time of Hogarth's famous canvas 'Gin Lane', and gin-selling had to be curbed by Government action. The noted distilling family of Nicholson operated here from 1872; distilling finally ending in 1941, as also the use of the old waterwheels.[3]

The Sugar Loaf

This has been written about as though it has entirely disappeared from this country. It did, commercially, when Martineaus ceased manufacture at Silvertown in 1897, as stated, but the story of the loaf did not end thus, as I had imagined. When preparing a talk on sugar history for the Hornchurch Historical Society, I was informed of a sugar loaf exhibited in the Castle Museum, York, a photograph of which was kindly prepared for me by the curator, Mr. R. Patterson, with the information that it was made in Czechoslovakia, was 2 ft. 2 ins. in height, weight 30 lbs., a large specimen. The photograph I submitted to *Tate and Lyle Times* with a request whether any other loaf existed in the country, but suggesting the York loaf was the only one. This had unexpected results, as with the magician's apprentice who started something larger than he anticipated. Replies[4] received revealed that a loaf, with cutters, was in the Folk Museum, Cambridge; as objects of curiosity were on the shelves of research centre, refiner's and broker's offices in London; they were sometimes prepared at Tate and Lyle's laboratories at Liverpool for Grocery Institutions, for Food and Brewers Exhibitions, for lectures, centenary celebrations, historic and ceremonial functions. The ancient custom of presenting sugar loaves to important personages has been perpetuated at Kingston-on-Thames. When a new Recorder, usually one eminent in legal circles, is installed at this royal borough, part of the proceedings is the presentation to him of two sugar loaves, and this ceremony was repeated in 1968[5] at the installation in the office of Sir F. Elwyn Jones, Q.C., then Attorney-General. An Essex interest is in the event, for he has been M.P. for West Ham South for several years, also the loaves were provided by Tate and Lyle, and several directors of that company were present. The loaves were 2 ft. high, 6 ins. across the base.

But not only for non-commercial purposes are sugar loaves still manufactured, for the correspondence that followed my magazine request revealed the existence of a large modern trade in them outside this country. The peoples of the Arabian Gulf, Northern Africa, Nigeria, Mauritania, consume annually some thousands of tons of sugar loaves, made in the Bordeaux refinery of Société Say, the Raffinerie Tirlemontoise of Belgium, both connected with Tate and Lyle, the Skrivany Raffineriede, Czechoslovakie, and others. The weights vary from 3 to 4½ lbs. approximately. The African-Arab peoples are not only conservative in habit, but also find these solid cones more portable on nomadic journeys than the usual packings of sugar. A very unexpected and gratifying result of my enquiries was the presentation to me of four sugar loaves by the Mincing Lane sugar brokers, E.D. and F. Man, who do business in this Continent-Arabian trade, the loaves coming from the three refineries above (two from Czechoslovakia). From this kind gift I re-donated a loaf each, with write up, to the Passmore Edwards Museum, Stratford, and the Havering Museum. Romford, in this way putting the sugar loaf on public display in Essex. One I keep for exhibition when giving talks on sugar history. Some changes in process have occurred. The old method (still operated in the 1874 refinery in chapter 3, using 'hot liquid sugar that flowed from taps') was to fill moulds with hot concentrated liquor that would crystallize and harden when drained and cold; at Liverpool, hot sugar paste or massecuite is used, to crystallize hard after clarifying and cooling, the comparatively small number allowing natural drainage of excess syrups; but the huge number produced by the Continental refineries makes this drainage by gravity impracticable on account of time and space, and at the Continental refineries the syrup is expelled by centrifugal machines (thanks to Marcel Delvany of Tirlemont for a communication concerning this). Noel Deerr, 1949-50, mentions this expelling.

Old London had 13 Sugar Loaf Courts, three Sugar Loaf Alleys, and two Sugar Loaf Yards,[6] some no doubt deriving their names from the many small sugar houses in the City during the 17th and 18th centuries. Of these little passages two remain. Garlick Hill has a Sugar Loaf Court (first mention 1708). At its entrance is the modest public house with its coloured p ainted sign, *The Crown and Sugar Loaf,* and not far away in Cannon Street is another public house, *The Sugar Loaf.* (*The Sugar Loaf* tavern in Great Queen Street has already been mentioned.)

The second survivor is Sugar Baker's Court (first mentioned 1677 as Sugar Baker's Yard) in Creechurch Lane, definitely indicating a former place of sugar refining, and again the sugar loaf appears close by in a metal sign of three gilt sugar loaves beneath a gilt crown outside the premises of Davison, Newman and Co. The origin of this firm, as teamen and grocers, dates back to 1650, and an early mention of the sign occurs in 1740.[7] The business has continued to the present day under the names of two 18th-century partners, but the fact that it was acquired in 1910 by the West Indian Produce Association is to some extent history repeating itself, for in 1789 the partners, Davison and Newman, bought a share in a Jamaican sugar plantation (as mentioned in chapter 5) and for 50 years imported sugar from thence. Tea and whisky are now the chief sales.

Born in Bethnal Green, I note with interest a Sugar Loaf Walk there, and through another birthplace with sugar connection we will by association return to Essex. The proprietor of a business listed in the South London telephone directory as 'Sugar Loaf Puppets' informed me he was born in Rio de Janeiro, near the Sugar Loaf Mountain, which suggested the name for his puppet-making establishment. The loaf name on such a grand scale connects with a South Hornchurch attic in which was found a number of ancient books dating from 1635. After due enquiries by the finder, I negotiated for him the sale of the books to the Bodleian Library, Oxford; among them was *The Lady's Complete Pocket Book for 1760* in which Amy Osman had written, 'I saw the Sugar Loaf Hill in Wales'.

A last note. From the windows of Tate and Lyle's new offices in Leon House, Croydon, can be 'picked out' the *Swan and Sugar Loaf* public house.[8] Old and new indeed make acquaintance. Also the old loaf still lingers in today's language, for my grocer tells me that some elderly customers ask for 'loaf sugar' when purchasing cubes.

The Vacuum Pan

What has been described as the most complete of inventions at the time of its birth is the vacuum pan, a second distinction that it was invented especially for the sugar industry,

although it is now used in many others. This remarkable
plant is worth some consideration, as many have been operated
in Essex, at Stratford and Felsted, but mostly of course in
Silvertown. Before the appearance of the vacuum pan in 1813
sugar solutions were boiled in open coppers or pans, requiring
much fuel, high boiling temperature, a lengthy period, and
much labour, added to which was the dark colouration caused
by excessive heat and some destruction of sucrose. The steam-
ing copper with the fire beneath was the rule for centuries.
It had become known that liquids boiled in a vacuum or partial
vacuum would boil at a lower temperature, the higher the
degree of vacuum the lower the boiling point. Some practical
way to boil large masses of liquid thus was studied by an apparently unlikely person, the Hon. Charles Howard, brother of
the 12th Duke of Norfolk but a clever chemist and engineer,
son-in-law to a sugar refiner and managing the refinery. He
invented a construction consisting of a sphere of metal, the
'pan', (a name perhaps carried over from the old open pans)
which communicated with a cylindrical vessel, the condenser,
the whole airtight. To the bottom of the condenser was
attached an extractor pump. The pump on starting withdrew
air from the two vessels, creating a vacuum, liquor was
admitted to the pan and heated. Some early pans had fires
underneath, later internal steam pipes provided heat. The
vapour emanating from the boiling mass, which if allowed to
accumulate would change vacuum into pressure, passed into
the condenser to meet a cascade of cold water, by which it was
condensed, leaving vacuum in its place, the condensing water
withdrawn by the extracting pump at the bottom of the condenser. So the operating proceeded, the boiling liquid sending
off vapour, the vapour condensed by cold water, creating vacuum, the water drawn out, together with air-leaks and air
from condensing water, by the pump. The liquid boiled cooler,
needed less heat, there was no discolouration or undesirable
action on the sugar, a great speeding-up of time. Such plant
and other new machinery were costly, explaining the fading
of the several small refineries into fewer larger businesses.

Because an adaption to the vacuum pan, that vessel of
prime importance in sugar processing, brought to Silvertown

its first refiner, some detailed description is given of this important innovation. By it James Duncan's firm produced its popular primrose-coloured sugar in succession to the duller yellow product by boiling the pan contents in a higher degree of vacuum than was the rule previously. How was that improved vacuum obtained? By taking advantage of an interesting physical phenomenon,[9] the introduction of which into a condenser was made the subject for a patent by an inventor, Davis, in 1828. A perfect vacuum will suspend in a tube 30 in. of mercury, though actually it is the external pressure of air balancing the column against the vacuum. More mercury added to the column displaces an equivalent amount from the bottom, the hieght kept constantly the same. With water, a much lighter medium, the suspended column is 35 ft., the height of the column varying in accordance with vacuum; the higher the degree of vacuum the higher the water column. The Duncan firm added a 35 ft. pipe to the bottom of the condenser, its lower end immersed in a tank of water (see illustration). As air was extracted from the condenser and vacuum created, water rose up the pipe, its level determined by the degree of vacuum above. Condenser water running on this column caused an equivalent displacement below, the height of the column was unaffected — an automatic discharge. Freed from the work of extracting water, the pump now became an airpump, which gave a better vacuum on the pan, a lower boiling point, the sugar of lighter shade. This innovation became known, even in the United States, as 'boiling Scotch'. Considering its benefits, its already established use, it seems odd that the first Lyle pans of 1883 did not have condensers with this 'atmospheric', 'barometric' or Torricellian pipe, as it was variously known (the last name after Torricelli, secretary to Galileo, and who first discovered how to produce vacuum). There was the unsatisfactory method of extracting condenser water and air by the same pump, which gave a low vacuum. 'The vacuum control was rudimentary' there was 'colour formation in the pans'. When in 1887 a fifth pan was added to the original four the atmospheric pipe changes were made.

Centrifugal Machine

Another invention, the effect of which was revolutionary, in more than one sense of the word, was the centrifugal machine. The familiar spin-drier used by the housewife illustrates its action, indeed it was invented in 1837 by Penzoldt for drying wool.[10] But it was applied and developed with remarkable success to sugar processing and as large numbers have been spinning day and night at Silvertown for over a century, and operate at Felsted, they are worth an extra comment. Their use is now indispensible whenever in the process occur crystals and syrup mixed in a paste, and the syrup has to be expelled. Before the centrifugal machine, this was done by simply allowing the syrup to drain out by gravity, whether raw sugar in hogsheads at the sugar cane factory, white sugar in the 'loaf' moulds, or other arrangements for gravitational draining. The machine reduced a matter of days to one of minutes, gave us 'granulated' sugar, made the affination process possible, cut out much that was prolonged, arduous and messy.

The first machines were driven from beneath, like the household spin-drier is at present, and the dried sugar had to be scooped out, but in 1852 a great name, Henry Bessemer of steel fame, comes into the story with a most valuable innovation, suspending the iron basket on a steel rod, so that the basket could be rotated by a pulley at the top of the rod. The bottom of the basket was detachable, and could be lifted up to allow the wall of dried sugar around the basket to be ploughed out into a receptacle below, saving an immense amount of labour. At the Great International Exhibition in the newly-constructed Crystal Palace, Sir Henry had his centrifugal machine on show in Class VI (manufacturing machines and tools) and was awarded a prize medal; a journalist's description is certainly vivid.[11] 'This formed an attractive display. The crystallized sugar with its adhesive coating of brown treacle was spun around in the wire cage at a speed of 1,800 revolutions per minute; on throwing a bowlful of cold water into the machine, in 30 seconds the dark, sticky mass was like a snowdrift, with its sparkling crystals compactly spread round the revolving basket. Crowds of people would stand round the machine, and seemed never tired of watching its operations'. Bessemer was largely responsible for putting the familiar 'granulated' sugar on our tables, and won awards for sugar-connected and other inventions, but fell down, great man as he was, on a sugar refinery that he built on the Thames to work a new process of his own conception; it was a failure, and the factory was shut down.

The beekeeper also uses the centrifugal machine, for the extraction of honey from the combs.

As for char, the decolourizing agent, a book could be written about it, remarked Sir Oliver Lyle. It has its Essex connotation with Hunt's Charcoal Ltd., of Sugar House Lane, Stratford, who at one time supplied such firms as Tate and Lyle, Martineaus, and Fowlers. Other decolouring methods are now, however, coming into use.

Perhaps I can end with the statement that sugar seems to have followed me in Essex. Some years ago I took up residence in then semi-rural Rainham, 10 miles by road from Silvertown. Housing development has brought on my left as neighbour a young draughtsman whose wife in her Irish girlhood topped sugar beet on a relative's farm during school holidays; a right-hand neighbour, who came from Kingston, Jamaica, some years ago; adjoining the bottom of my garden is that of a promoted panman of Tate and Lyle; and opposite across the road lives the supervisor of the Company's telephone switchboard in Mincing Lane; and now my grandson, also of the same road, is to marry the daughter of a member of the laboratory staff at Thames Refinery.

SOURCES OF INFORMATION

Abbreviations:

E.R.O. Essex Record Office.
B.M.   British Museum. Department of Printed Books.
Inf.   Information.

CHAPTER I

1. Judges XIV, O.T.
2. Oliver Lyle, *The Plaistow Story*, (1960), Tate & Lyle, London.
3. *Beekeeping in Antiquity*, 2nd edn. (1960), University of London.
   History of Beekeeping in Britain, (1958), Bee Research Assn., London.
   These two books by H. Malcolm Fraser have been very helpful.
4. This and other inf., with a personal visit, from W.E. Hooper, County Beekeeping Instructor.
5. G. Chell, Readers' Letters, *Essex Countryside*, No. 163 (Aug. 1970), p.58.
6. *Essex Beekeepers Assoc. Magazine*, (July, 1967).
7. *Victoria County History of Essex*, Vol. 2, p.366.
8. J. Timbs, *Something for Everybody*, (1866). London.
9. Alfred Hills, 'Bee Superstitions', *Essex Review*, Vol. 34 (Oct. 1925), pp.218-9: Charlotte C. Mason, 'Witchcraft and Magic in Essex', *Essex Review*, Vol. 37 (April, 1928) pp.63-6.
10. E.R.O.
11. R. Webb, Essex Beekeepers Assoc.
12. Mr. J.A. Hugill, for Conrad quotation.

CHAPTER II

1. Margaret Labarge, *A Baronial Household of the 13th Century* (1965), Eyre and Spottiswoode, London.
2. J. Lindsay, *The Discovery of Britain* (1949), London.
3. E.R.O.
4. J.C. Cox, *Churchwardens' Accounts* (1913) p.36. London.
5. F.G. Emmison, *Tudor Secretary* (1970) Phillimore & Co., London. Other inf. received from him.

6.   A. Searle, 'Sir Thomas Barrington in London, 1640-1644', *Essex Journal*, Vol. 2, No. 2 (March, 1967) p.63.
7.   E.R.O.
8.   T.M.H., 'Some pages from an old rent book', *Essex Review*, Vol. 33 (1924) pp.204-8.
9.   F. Cornwell, inf.
10.   D. Wickham (Thurrock Librarian), inf.
11.   Revd. G.T. Townsend, *The Siege of Colchester*, S.P.C.K., London.
12.   T. Cromwell, *Historic Towns, Colchester* (1825), London.
13.   P. Morant, *History and Antiquities of the County of Essex*, (Published London, 1768, reprinted Colchester, 1816). Other works consulted, Noel Deerr, *The History of Sugar* (1949): L.G.A. Strong, *The Story of Sugar* (1954).

CHAPTER III

1.   Oliver Lyle, *Technology of Sugar for Refinery Workers*, 2nd edn. (1950), London.
2.   Dorothy Davis, *A History of Shopping* (1966), London.
3.   Revd. Herbert Brown, *History of St. Lawrence Parish* (1928), Chelmsford.
4.   Dorothy Davis, op. cit.
5.   G. Martineau, *Sugar*, revised F. Eastick, 6th edn., (1932). Pitman, London.
6.   J. Shawcross, *History of Dagenham* (1904), London.
7.   Stratford Library, inf.
8.   Ilford Central Library, inf. Other inf. from Ilford Library.
9.   C.T. Perfect, *Ye Olde Village of Hornchurch* (1917), Colchester.
10.   *City Press Supplement*, 5.4.1963.
11.   P. Gifford, Colchester Librarian, inf.
12.   James Greenwood, *The Wilds of London* (1874), Chatto & Windus, London.
13.   Millicent Rose, *The East End of London* (1951), Cresset Press London.
14.   W.R. Aykroyd, *Sweet Malefactor, Sugar, Slavery and Human Society* (1967). W. Heinemann, London.
15.   Inf. from Port of London Authority.
16.   O. Lyle, *Technology of Sugar for Refinery Workers*.

CHAPTER IV

1.   *Dictionary of National Biography*, Clarendon Press, Oxford.
2.   Sir C. Firth and G. Davies, *Regimental History of Cromwell's Army* (1940) Clarendon Press, Oxford.
3.   Said to be near *The George*.

4.   George Caunt, 'The Monks of New Hall', *Essex Countryside*,
        No. 80, (Sep. 1963) pp.471-3.

5.   Michael Lewis, *History of the British Navy* (1959), George
        Allen and Unwin, London.

6.   C.V. Black, *The Story of Jamaica* (1965) London.

7.   S.A. Chase, 'Training Ships of Thurrock', *Thurrock Hist. Soc.
        Journal* (1960), Book 5, pp.3-4.

8.   Michael Lewis, *op. cit.*

9.   Dr. Eric Williams, *Capitalism and Slavery* (1964) Andre
        Deutsch, London.

10.   *House of Commons Session Papers*, 1837-8, Vol. 40. B.M.

11.   Gladys Amy Ward, *History of South Weald and Brentwood*
        (1961), privately printed.

12.   G.W. Howe, 'The Two Harveys of Hempstead (2)', *Essex
        Countryside*, No. 70 (November, 1942) p.30.

13.   C.V. Black, *op. cit.*

14.   Revd. W.H. Taylor, Southminster, inf.

CHAPTER V

1.   *Dictionary of National Biography.*

2.   A. Mee, *Essex* (1966), Hodder and Stoughton, London.

3.   C. Nicole, *The West Indies* (1965), Hutchinson, London.

4.   John Atkins, *A Voyage to Guinea, Brazil and the West Indies*
        (1735). B.M.

5.   I. Sparkes, 'Jeremiah Dummer and Yale College Library', *Essex
        Journal*, Vol. 2, No. 3 (June 1967) pp.160-4.

6.   Bernard Martin, *John Newton, A Biography*, A revised edn.
        (1960), Epworth Press, London.

7.   D.P. Mannix in collaboration with M. Cowley, *Black Cargoes*
        (1963), Longmans, London.

8.   L. Thompson, D. Wickham (Thurrock Librarian), inf.

9.   D/DM. F27/8

10.   *The Story of Upminster* (1957). Compiled by members of
        Upminster local history study group. Book 5, pp.1,8.

11.   O. Rutter, *At the Three Sugar Loaves and Crown* (1938),
        Davison, Newman and Co., London.

12.   E.R.O. *Estate and Family Archives.*
        "   A.C. Edwards, *English History from Essex Sources.*
        "   W. Barry, *Pedigrees of Essex Families.*

13.   W. Beckford, Junior. *Remarks . . . Negroes in Jamaica* (1788).
        B.M.

14.   R. Pares, *A West India Fortune* (1950), Longmans, Green &
        Co., London.

CHAPTER VI

1. G. Harper, 'The Mashams of Otes,' *Essex Countryside*, No. 102, p.571.
2. R.V. Holt, *The Unitarian Contribution to Social Progress in England* (1951), Lindsey Press, London.
3. F. Lewis, *The Tayler Memorial Lecture* (1935). Privately published.
4. Sir Jerome Murch, *Memoir of Robert Hibbert, Esquire* (1874), privately printed, Bath.
5. E. Williams, *Capitalism and Slavery* (1964), Andre Deutsch, London.
6. R. Barrett-Lennard, Readers' Letters, *Essex Countryside*, No. 149 (June, 1967) p.47.
7. Revd. D. Graebe, Great Parndon, inf.
8. Leslie Thompson, *The Land that Fanns* (1957), Chelmsford.
9. Lucy Sutherland, *A London Merchant* (1962), Frank Cass & Co., London.
10. Sir Edward Buxton, M.P. Parliamentary Motion on State of West India Colonies, *Annual Register* (1850), p.51.
11. J. Curwen, *Old Plaistow*, 4th edn. (1905), Plaistow.
12. Carola Oman, *The Gascoyne Heiress, the Life and Diaries of Frances Mary Gascoyne-Cecil, 1802-39* (1968), Hodder and Stoughton, London. The family name of Gascoyne was later changed to Gascoigne.
13. C. Black, *The Story of Jamaica*: Mannix and Cowley, *Black Cargoes*: A. Waugh, *A Family of Islands*.

CHAPTER VII

1. F. Sainsbury, M.B.E. and Mrs. D. Taylor, of the Stratford Library, much inf.
2. J. Curwen, in obituary notice, *Int. Sugar Journal* (1905), Vol. 7, p.563.
3. A. Crouch, *Silvertown and Neighbourhood* (1900), London.
4. Shaftesbury Society, inf.
5. D. Reid, County Librarian, Dunoon, inf.
6. A.J. Fairrie, photographs of memorial in *Tate and Lyle Times*, Christmas 1958, January, 1959.
7. J. Curwen, *op. cit.*
8. Henry Tate Centenary publication.
9. O. Lyle, *The Plaistow Story*.
10. G. Fairie, *The Refining Families of Great Britain*, (1951) Tate and Lyle.
11. Appearing in *The East End of London*, Millicent Rose.
12. Mr. P. Martineau, inf.
13. *Stratford Express*, 17.6.1893.

CHAPTER VIII

1.   O. Lyle, *The Plaistow Story*, on which publication much of this chapter is based.
2.   *The Grocer*, 5.5.1883.
3.   O. Lyle, op. cit.
4.   Ibid.
5.   In *Tate and Lyle Times*, (1967).
6.   O. Lyle.
7.   J. Parsons, *A Short History of Queen Mary's Hospital for the East End* (1962), West Ham Group Hospitals, London.
8.   Capt. O.K. Williams, Personnel Supt., Sugar Line, inf.
9.   *Tate and Lyle Times*, (several issues).
10. Ibid.

CHAPTER IX

1.   W. Aykroyd, *Sweet Malefactor*.
2.   E.R.O. Tithes Apportionment List, 1838. D/CT/372 A. & B.
3.   M. Christy, *Essex Review*, Vol. XII.
4.   *V.C.H. Essex* (1907), Vol. 2, p.591.
5.   Inf. from Mr. J. Payne, Ulting Hall.
6.   *Journal of Friends Historical Society*. XII, 1915.
7.   N. Deerr, *History of Sugar*.
8.   As Note 6 above.
9.   *Illustrated London News* (15.11.1851). (Also quoted by Caroline Tate, *Tate and Lyle Times*, April, 1968.)
10. Mr. C. Anderson, 'Lavenham Receivers' in *Tate and Lyle Times*, Sept. 1964. Other inf. received from him.
11. V.C.H. Essex, Vol. 5, p.216.
12. *Report on Sugar Beet Industry,* Ministry of Agriculture and Fisheries (1931).
13. C.H. Warren, *Essex* (1950), London.
14. S.M. Jarvis, 'Essex Grows Sugar', *Essex Countryside*, No. 93. (Oct. 1963) pp.582-4.
15. Rev. Major P. Wright, Series 'Down on the Essex farm', *Essex Countryside*, Nos. 52, 71, 75, 84, 112.

CHAPTER X

1.   J. Garbutt, *A Hundred Years of Progress* (1955). A copy in Patent Office Library, London.
2.   Ind Coope, visitors' booklet.
3.   Miss E. Gardner, *The Three Mills, Bromley-by-Bow* (1957). Society for the Protection of Ancient Buildings, London.

4. *Tate and Lyle Times* Dec. 1968. Feb., Mar., Aug. 1969.
5. Librarian and Curator, Kingston-on-Thames, inf.
6. H. Harben, *Dictionary of London* (1918), London.
7. O. Rutter, *At the Three Sugar Loaves and Crown.*
8. Mr. H. Shaw, Leon House, inf.
9. G. Martineau and F. Eastick, *Sugar.*
10. O. Lyle, *Technology for Sugar Refinery Workers.*
11. *Illustrated London News* 8.11.1851.

APPENDIX

During the unavoidable delay in publishing this book certain facts have emerged worth inclusion in an appendix. Our entry into the Comcom Market has exerted an adverse effect on cane-sugar refining in this country, and could make sugar a minor activity among the more profitable ones taken up by the Tate and Lyle Group. The now large Manbre and Garton Group include Martineaus Ltd., though the former Company engaged in cane-sugar refining and packet sugar after absorbing the Sankey Company in 1935. To clarify a point about 'other sugars' in Chapter X — the starch which is converted into glucose is derived from imported maize.

The statement in Chapter III that all of the East End refining buildings have disappeared needs qualification. The *London Advertiser* for 19th October 1972 describes the destructive fire at the Monastery Bonded Tea Warehouse in Dock Street, Whitechapel, and goes on to state that this nine-storey building, built in the early half of the 19th century, was formerly a sugar refinery, built by French prisoners-of-war during the Napoleonic era, and was listed as a building of historic or archaeological interest. The Guildhall Library furnished me with a list of sugar-refiners owning the business to 1874, after which year it became a tea warehouse. A recent visit showed the building to have walls intact with iron supporting pillars inside, and that it can be made fit for use again.

Chapter V. To the list of Essex owners of sugar plantations can be added a remarkable example of how undoubted humanitarian principles in one sphere could co-exist with living on an income connected with slave labour. Sir W. Hillary, the virtual founder of the Royal National Lifeboat Institution, which is celebrating the 150th anniversary of its beginning (1824) inherited large West Indian estates. He came into possession of Danbury Place, Essex through eloping with the heiress. While here he was awarded a baronetcy for organising defence corps during the Napoleonic invasion scare. But as the war continued the collapse of West Indian trade, and the failure of his sugar crop caused him to assume more modest living in Douglas, Isle of Man. His participation in the lifeboat activities here led him to perceive the great need of an organised life-saving service on a national scale, and his published pamphlet in 1833 urging this attracted influential notice, resulting in the founding of what is now the familiar R.N.L.I.

16th March 1974   FRANK LEWIS

INDEX

Abbey Mills, 116

Admirals, Essex: Barrington, Samuel, 42-43; Benbow, John, 40-41; Harvey, Eliab, 44-45; Jervis, John, 43-44; Penn, Sir William, 36. Others: Knowles, Charles 41-42; Nelson, Lord 43, 44, 45; Vernon, Edward, 41-42

Atkins, John, 48-50, 63

Ayloffe, Sir Benjamin, 22

Beckford, George (ex-panman) 58-59; William (Alderman), 58-59; William (Junior) 59-60

Beehive 'Village', 10-11

Beekeeping, Ancient, 2, 3, 4, 5; modern, 7-9, 10, 12 -13

Bees, St. Ambrose, 2; boles, 4-5; early mention, 1-2; telling the bees, 7, 8-9; toxic sprays, 8,11 -12

Beet Sugar, British Sugar Corporation, 107; continental bounties, 104, 105, 106, 107; early mention, 100, 106; Lavenham 104; McArdle, Mrs., 110-111; Tate and Lyle, 107, 110; (see Ulting and Felsted)

Berry, Albert, E., 112-115

Brown, A.C., 4, 10

Cane Sugar, Early mention, 14-18, 20; increased production, 18, 21, 23-24; process developments, 20, 25, 32, 77, 82, 89; vacuum pan, 119-121; centrifugal machine, 122-123

Cherry Garden, 73-75

Clyde Wharf (shipping) 96-97

Colchester, 17, 21-22, 29, 62

Conrad, Joseph, 13

Cornwall, H.M.S. and T.S. 41-42

Cromwell, Oliver, 35, 36, 38

Curwen, Revd., J. Spencer, 26, 40, 77, 82

Defoe, Daniel, 38, 62

Dickens, Charles, 25, 79, 92

Duncan, James, Clyde Wharf Refinery, 77, 81, 121; Lavenham Beet, 104, 107; Personal notes, 77-81

Felsted, 107-111, 120

Gascogne (later Gascoigne), Bamber (Barking) 72; Mary, Lady, 72

Hibbert, Robert, 65-66

Liverpool, 22, 53, 65, 70, 72, 82, 84, 98, 117, 118

Lyle, Abram (founder) 88; Charles, son of Abram, 88, 94; C.E. Leonard (1st Baron of Westbourne), 90-91, 95; Charles (2nd Baron), Foreword, 94; Oliver, Sir, 90-91, 95; John Oliver (Chairman) 95; Plaistow Wharf Refinery, T.L. Group) 76, 83-94, 97-99, 107, 121

Langtons (Hornchurch), Holmes, Colonel, 27, 28; Vagener, John, 27; Williams, Varco, 28

Manbre and Garton, 86, 114

Martineau, Clyde Wharf, 84-85, David and Sons, 84-86, George

82, 86; James (Unitarian divine), 86-87
Mead, 2, 6, 13
Monck, Christopher (Duke of Albemarle), 39
Murder at Silvertown, 33-34

Pepys, Samuel, 37
Petre, Sir William, 16-17

Refineries, early, London, 20, 24, 29-32; Stratford, 28-29, 120
Refiners living in Essex, 24, 25-28

Scott, Revd. A, 45
Slavery, negro, for sugar plantations, 38, 46-61, 70, (abolition, 71)
Slavery, opposition to, Buxton, Samuel, F., 70-71, 72; Clarkson, Thomas, 65, 70; Cooke, George, 53; Forster, Benjamin, 71; Johnson, Samuel, 63; Locke, John, 62; Sharp, Granville, 63, 69-70; Wesley, John, 63; Wilberforce, William, 65, 70, 71, 72; (see Unitarians)
Slave owners, Essex, Ames, Mrs., 61; Conyers, John, 55-56; Esdaile, Sir J., 54; Jessup, Edward, 60; Mathew, Hon. W. 55; Mathew, William, 55; Tysen, William, 57; Pinney, John (friend of Jessup) 60-61
Slave Traders, Essex, Lodge, Thomas, 46-47; Newton, John, 51-53; Oglethorpe, James, 48, 66; (see Atkins)
Slave servants in Essex, 66-69
Society of Friends, 64, 70, 72
Sugar, Adulteration, 24; Neighbouring Essex, Albion Sugar Co., 115-116; Fowler Ltd., 115, 123; Thames Traffic, 28, 32; (see Beet and Cane)
Sugar brokers, Cumberland House, 34; E.D. & F. Man, 118

Tate, Francis, H., 84; Henry, Sir, 82-84; Thames Refinery, 82-83, 99
Tate and Lyle, 75, 82, 95, 96, 97 99, 117, 118, 123
Tate Gallery, 83
Tokens, 18-19

Ulting, 101
Unitarianism, 63-66, 82, 84, 103, 1
Unitarians opposing Slavery, Rathbone, William, 65; Roscoe, William, 64, 65; Smith, William, M.P., 65; Wedgwood, Josiah, 64

West Indies, 20, 30-37, 38-39 66, 71, 73, 96, 97, 119
Whittier, John, 2, 8

Young, Arthur, 23-24